I0037028

DEATH OF THE
STRESS TEST

BEYOND THE RESULTS:
Decades Of
Misdirection

BY

DIAMOND FERNANDES

Copyright © 2025 by Diamond Fernandes

All rights reserved.

No part of this publication may be reproduced, stored in a retrieval system, or transmitted in any form or by any means—electronic, mechanical, photocopying, recording, or otherwise—without the prior written permission of the copyright holder, except in the case of brief quotations used in critical articles or reviews.

This book is a work of non-fiction. The information presented herein is intended for educational and informational purposes only. While every effort has been made to ensure accuracy, the author and publisher assume no responsibility for errors or omissions. The reader is encouraged to consult a qualified professional for medical, legal, or financial advice.

i

TABLE OF CONTENTS

ACKNOWLEDGEMENTS

I want to thank my loved ones who have stood beside me on this journey. Your support, patience, and sacrifices have given me the space to pursue this work. I do this not just for myself, but for the experiences we share together.

To my colleagues, mentors, and peers I want to thank you for your wisdom and guidance over the years. You've sharpened my thinking and helped me grow into the clinician, and author I strive to be.

And to my patients, you are the heart of this book. You've entrusted me with your stories, your struggles, and your hopes. Your courage inspires me, and your "beautiful hearts" remind me daily why this mission matters. Thank you for allowing me to walk with you on the path of preventing and reversing heart disease.

PREFACE

The stress test has become a rite of passage in cardiology.

It's simple, safe, and widely available. No radiation. No injections. No surgical risk. Just a treadmill, a few wires, and a screen, watching to see how your heart performs under pressure. Even outside of medicine, the phrase "stress test" has become part of our everyday vocabulary. Financial systems get stress-tested. Organizations do simulations. It's a concept that suggests clarity: let's see where the cracks are before something breaks.

And in theory, that's what cardiac stress testing was hoping to do.

I've performed thousands of them. I know the drill. The consent form, where we explain that the risk of a serious event is roughly 1 in 10,000. The cautious optimism in a patient's eyes as they step onto the treadmill. The quiet calculation in a clinician's mind, looking for electrocardiogram changes or symptoms.

But during my first year in this field of cardiac health, I experienced that "1 in 10,000" moment.

It happened. Right in front of me.

A patient collapsed mid-test. Full code blue. I watched a cardiologist leap across the room to deliver a life-saving shock, a blur of paddles, protocol, adrenaline. Thankfully, that patient survived. But something in me shifted.

Because despite the rarity of that moment, what shook me more was what I saw over the years that followed.

Patient after patient walked away from a "normal" stress test, reassured that everything looked fine, only to return weeks or months later with a heart attack. Others failed the test and rushed into stents or bypass surgery, believing it saved their lives, only to find out later that those procedures didn't reduce their future risk or change the course of their disease.

And yet, we keep repeating the cycle.

We keep ordering a test that misses the majority of heart attacks, that leads to invasive interventions with limited benefit in stable patients, and that too often provides false reassurance when vigilance was needed most.

That's why I wrote this book.

To challenge the default. To explain the science. And to offer a smarter, biology-based way to detect, understand, and prevent cardiovascular disease, before the emergency.

If you are a patient who's been told your heart is fine because your test was "normal," this book is for you. If you are a patient who has a failed stress test, this book is for you.

If you're a clinician who wonders whether the tools we use are still serving us, or just serving tradition, this book is for you too.

Because what we need isn't just a better test. We need a better model.

And the journey to that model starts with seeing stress testing, not as a villain, but as a symptom. A symptom of how cardiology has become reactive, not proactive. How we've focused on what's easy to see, instead of what truly matters. And how we've missed the biology beneath the blockage.

This is a book about that biology. And it's time we start paying attention to it.

I've been given the gift of a second life. It began the moment I understood I only get one. That clarity led me to help others prevent and reverse heart disease before it's too late. With every patient who faces a life-threatening diagnosis, I'm reminded of what matters most: the desire to keep doing what we love with the people we love.

My mission is to inspire and empower through transformative ideas so that what is possible is realized.

CHAPTER 1 — The Roundtable That Said Too Much

It's funny how you can walk into a room expecting collaboration… and walk out realizing you need to write a book.

That room was a boardroom at the Libin Heart Institute of Calgary, and the topic was serious: cardiac over-testing in Alberta. Between 2008 and 2018, there had been a parabolic increase in cardiovascular testing, far outpacing any population growth. The public system was overwhelmed. The evidence didn't support the volume. And yet, the machine kept running.

I was invited to be part of the solution.

The meeting brought together cardiologists, internal medicine physicians, radiologists, and cardiac rehab professionals. I'd spent my career in this field, building a preventive cardiology clinic, mentoring under Calgary's best cardiologists, attending every Canadian Cardiovascular Congress since 1999, and serving on the executive board of the Canadian Association of Cardiovascular Prevention and Rehabilitation.

This was my world.

At the time of the meeting, I was already sitting on the national board. A few years later, I'd go on to become president of CACPR (2022–2024). I say this not to boast, but to give context: I wasn't an outsider at this table. I was and am deeply invested in the future of cardiovascular care in Canada.

But that day, I had to have some tough skin.

As I entered the room, I made my usual rounds, introducing myself and connecting with familiar faces. A few seats down, an internal medicine physician I had known for years, someone I had once even considered going into business with, sat quietly. Until he didn't.

In front of a dozen physicians, he launched into a public censure.

"You failed my patient," he said, referring to a decision I made not to refer one of his patients for additional cardiac testing.

"You're ruining my patient care."

Now, I've been doing this long enough to handle tension, but this wasn't professional disagreement, this was an attack. Calmly, I said,

"I'm sure I had a reason. Let's discuss it after the meeting."

But he pressed on.

He explained how he refers to the publicly funded cardiac rehab program in Calgary, as if the Heart Fit Clinic didn't qualify. I reminded him respectfully, that we are in fact an accredited cardiac rehabilitation program. I explained my role on the national board, and how I have helped shape standards of care across the country. Still, he dismissed it.

And then he said this:

"You're too aggressive in your communication."

I didn't flinch.

"I'm just telling the truth."

That was the moment I realized something important: the truth is considered aggressive when it threatens the system's comfort.

Because here's the truth:

We are over-testing patients with tools that don't catch early disease.

We are giving people a "clean bill of health" based on tests that miss 90% of risk.

We are letting financial incentives drive clinical decisions, consciously or unconsciously.

And we are ignoring the deeper biology of heart disease in favour of a plumbing model that no longer fits.

The actual meeting focused on how to reduce unnecessary testing. The Choosing Wisely campaign was mentioned, a national initiative to cut down on procedures that offer little value. But when it came time to choose what to cut, nobody wanted to touch stress testing, arguably the most outdated and misused cardiac tool in circulation.

Instead, they proposed we start with easy targets like routine ECGs and Holter monitors. We'd reconvene in six months.

I left the room frustrated. But also, curious. If everyone agrees we're testing too much, and if stress testing is the gateway to so much unnecessary follow-up, why is no one willing to address it?

So, I did what I always do when something doesn't sit right: I dug in.

I began collecting studies, analyzing outcomes, cross-referencing patient cases, and reviewing decades of data. The result is what you're holding in your hands.

This isn't a book written in anger, though it was sparked by frustration. It's written in service. In service of patients who trust the system. In service of doctors who feel trapped in it. And in service of a future where heart disease is detected before it becomes a crisis, not after.

This book is about truth, and if telling the truth is "too aggressive," so be it.

Because what I can't live with is silence

CHAPTER 2 – The Game That Nearly Cost Me My Life

It was a snowy, cold Family Day weekend in Calgary, the kind of morning where everything moves a little slower. The roads were covered, the wind had bite, and I woke up just… off. Not sick, but not sharp. Not in pain, but not myself.

Normally, I'm the guy who's out shoveling the driveway the moment the snow starts to settle, especially with the way it ices up around here. But that morning, I couldn't bring myself to do it. I just didn't have the energy.

I chalked it up to lingering post-COVID fatigue. I'd had it back in December, and I figured maybe I hadn't fully bounced back. Still, I didn't think much of it. I had tickets to the Flames game with my boys, and they were excited.

We bundled up, loaded into the car, and headed downtown. The excitement in the car was real, my boys were bouncing. It felt like a good distraction. A reset.

We parked, made our way into the Saddledome, and started the familiar climb up to the seats.

That's when it hit me.

Just a few flights of stairs. Nothing extreme. Normally, I'd take them two at a time without even thinking. But that day, I felt a tightening in my chest. I was short of breath. My heart started to pound, not just fast, but wrong. The rhythm wasn't normal. It was fluttering. Offbeat. Atrial fibrillation? SVT (Supra-Ventricular Tachycardia)? PVCs (Premature Ventricular Contractions)?

This is what I do for a living, I know these rhythms. And I knew right then something was wrong.

I made it to my seat and sat down. Caspian, my middle son, looked at me.

"Are you okay?"

I looked at him and said, "Hey buddy... you might have to go home with your uncle. I might need to go to Emergency."

His face tightened.

"What should we do? Should I call Mom? Where do we go? What's happening?"

I'm the heart guy. How could this be happening to me?

I calmed myself down. I took deep, timed breaths. Slowly. Carefully. The rhythm settled. My pulse slowed. I knew I wasn't having a heart attack. But something was clearly off.

We stayed for the rest of the game. But I kept calm. I love cheering the Flames on, but not that day.

I was quiet, subdued. I didn't even lift my youngest when he climbed into my lap. I just sat still and focused, monitoring every single beat.

Something Was Still Wrong

When we got home, I slowly climbed the stairs, just one flight. Normally I'd bounce up two steps at a time, light and fast. This time, I had to stop midway. Shortness of breath. Chest pressure.

But the timing couldn't have been worse.

I was in the middle of a major insurance application, something I'd been working on for months. Meetings, paperwork, calls, medical requirements. I'd jumped through every hoop. The finish line was in sight.

I remember thinking, let me just get this over with. I've come this far. Let me finish it.

That's how we think, isn't it? We downplay symptoms, delay action, and hope we can outrun whatever's catching up to us.

But then Caspian was concerned, told my wife what happened at the hockey game. She didn't hesitate. She called a close friend, physicians, and within minutes, an ambulance pulled up to our house.

I was still calm. My heart rhythm had settled again. My vitals were stable. My ECG was normal. No signs of a heart attack.

But I didn't feel okay.

And then my wife said something that cut

through everything:

"I don't care about the insurance. We can't play with this. This is an emergency."

She was right. That moment reset my perspective. It wasn't about paperwork, timelines, or the illusion of control. It was about listening, really listening to my body.

The ER Visit: I Knew What They'd Say

The emergency physician was kind, attentive, and professional, working through the steps just as he'd been trained to do. And to be fair, I wasn't making it easy. By the time I got there, my rhythm had settled. Whatever had happened at the hockey game, the shortness of breath, the palpitations climbing those stairs, it had passed. My heart rate was calm now. My breathing was steady.

He started with the ECG. It looked normal, no arrhythmia, no ST elevation. I knew exactly what he was looking for: dangerous rhythms, signs of ischemia, or worse, a full-blown heart attack, what we call a STEMI (ST Elevation Myocardial Infarction). But nothing showed up. Just a clean tracing. Quiet.

Next came the bloodwork. Troponins were normal, no elevation to suggest active heart muscle injury. Cardiac enzymes were stable. My vitals were right where they should be. Blood pressure, heart rate, oxygen saturation, all giving the illusion of calm.

It was textbook emergency medicine, and he did it well. He was polite, focused, and followed the playbook with confidence. And I sat there, patient and agreeable. I knew how hard his job was. But inside, it took everything in me not to speak up, because I'd seen this scenario before, too many times. I'd seen patients discharged when something didn't feel right... because on paper, everything looked fine.

And now I was that patient. I didn't want to overstep. I didn't want to interrupt. But I also knew this couldn't end here.

He looked at me and said the words so many patients are relieved to hear:

"You're good to go."

And I get it. That's the protocol. If you're not in an active cardiac emergency, they're trained to clear you and move to the next patient.

But then I asked him for his stethoscope.

I placed it on my chest and listened, and what I heard wasn't panic. It was a wave of fear.

And I heard it.

A violent wave, a murmur.

He listened again. "Yeah," he said. "I hear it too. Likely nothing. Maybe a follow-up in clinic."

A sound I knew didn't belong. A sound he was dismissing.

He listened again. He heard it too. He shrugged a little, unsure, and suggested it was probably nothing.

At some point in this conversation, I finally told him what I do, that I work in cardiovascular risk, that this is my world, that I didn't just wander in here guessing.

It wasn't about ego. It was about urgency. And thankfully, he understood.

He came back to my bedside and said: "Good news! The cardiologist will see you in his clinic in two weeks."

"I'm supposed to go ski touring in a few days," I told him. "I'm already here. Let's not wait. This is urgent."

He left and returned with a revised plan: an urgent echocardiogram at 8 a.m. the next morning.

But I couldn't help thinking:

What if I hadn't known what to ask for? What if I didn't push? What if I'd gone home… like most people would?

Emergency physicians are trained to respond to patterns, to rule out life-threatening conditions with proven protocols. And for that, they're amazing. But they're not trained to look beyond the checklist. They don't often have time, context, or capacity to ask why something doesn't add up when all the boxes are ticked.

That night, I wasn't in full-blown crisis. But I was on the edge of one. And I was almost missed, not because of negligence, but because I didn't fit the model they're built to respond to.

The Long Night in a Hospital Chair

But there was no bed. Just a chair that reclined like an airplane seat and this was my bed for the night.

I spent the night upright in that chair; exhausted, anxious, trying to sleep under with all the beeps and chatter going on with nurses coming and going. No pain. No palpitations. But no peace, either. They woke me up and I surprisingly felt good, so I was expecting something not as bad.

At 8 a.m., I portered into the echocardiogram suite. I happened to know the tech from my Total Cardiology days.

Part of me still thought this would turn out to be minor. A fluke. A harmless murmur. Maybe a small leak.

Instead, I was told I had a flailing mitral valve caused by a ruptured chordae tendineae, a structural issue, not electrical or plumbing. The valve was whipping wildly with every beat.

And the verdict?

Open heart surgery. Immediately.

Knowing My Heart — From the Inside

I wasn't supposed to be here. I eat well. I

exercise. I know my numbers. I run a heart clinic. I help people prevent these emergencies.

But after that initial echo revealed a flailing mitral valve, the next steps moved quickly. They needed confirmation. The cardiology team ordered a transesophageal echocardiogram (TEE), a more invasive procedure where an ultrasound probe is passed down the esophagus for clearer images of the heart's internal structures.

The TEE confirmed it: flail leaflet, ruptured chordae. Structural failure. Not rhythm. Not plumbing.

Still, the team didn't yet know what kind of open-heart surgery I would need. That depended on whether I had any coronary artery disease. Were they going to crack my sternum open or do a minimally invasive surgery through my rib cage. So, the final test they ordered was a CT angiogram, an imaging scan to visualize the arteries and assess for blockages before surgery.

I had never had a CT angiogram before. Truthfully, I've always advised against using it as a screening tool, too much radiation for something that still sees arteries like pipes. But now, this was a surgical planning tool and to see if I have artery disease. And I felt confident. After all, I've done all the preventive testing at my clinic. My markers had always been good.

I even asked the tech to share the images with me when they were done. I was looking forward to confirming what I already knew: no blockages.

But once I was on the table, lying flat, arms above my head, heart beating under a failing valve, something changed.

They asked me to hold my breath. Then breathe out and hold again. I tried. But I couldn't.

I looked up at the screen above me, and there it was. Atrial fibrillation. My heart couldn't handle the maneuver. The rhythm went wild. I could feel the dysfunction ripple through my chest.

I told them to stop the test. I asked, "Do we really need this?" The only other option was a conventional angiogram, through the groin, threading a catheter all the way to the coronary arteries. This is a test that should be done only for emergencies and heart attacks. The radiation exposure did not excite me at all.

I really didn't want that. But after a lot of discussion, I gathered myself. I went back in to finish the CT angiogram.

They added the contrast. My heart flipped again, right back into atrial fibrillation. I felt it, and I saw it happen in real time.

They quickly pulled me out and said, "We got what we needed."

The First Time I Knew I Was Really Sick

That was the moment it truly hit me, I was sick. Really sick.

This wasn't just a murmur. This wasn't just a

valve issue. My heart was struggling to function. Every movement, every breath, was now something I had to manage.

The good news? The CT angiogram confirmed I had no coronary artery disease. That was a small but deeply affirming victory. Everything I'd built my clinic around, lifestyle, prevention, and advanced testing, had held up. There were no blockages. My father having artery disease was something I was doing my best to avoid.

That meant I was eligible for the minimally invasive surgical approach instead of having my sternum cracked open. But "minimally invasive" doesn't mean "minimal pain."

Recovery — And Remembering Nothing

I don't remember much about the first four days after surgery. I was intubated in the ICU and had a rough time coming off sedation. Those were blurry hours, filled with tubes, beeping monitors, and vague memories that don't quite stitch together.

When I was finally moved to recovery, I felt like I'd been hit by a bus.

But I was alive. I had survived.

I had been caught, not by the system, but by my own persistence… and by listening to my body.

I was flooded with emotion. Messages from family. From friends. From patients. From colleagues.

And I knew, in that moment, something I'd always believed, but now felt in my bones:

I am here for something bigger.

The Bigger Lesson

There are three systems in the heart:

Electrical – rhythm, arrhythmias, pacing issues.

Structural – valves, muscle function, chamber size.

Plumbing – arteries, blockages, blood flow.

Cardiology is built for emergencies. If you're having a heart attack, they will save your life.

But when you're not having a heart attack... when it's electrical or structural... when it's not showing up on a stress test or ECG... you can fall through the cracks.

And if I, a heart health professional, who knew what was happening, who knew how to advocate, who knew what tests to ask for, if I almost got missed...

What about everyone else?

This Book Is for That

This isn't just a memoir of a misdiagnosis. It's not just a story of a snowy day and a close call.

It's a call to rethink how we detect, interpret, and prevent heart disease.

Because not every heart problem is a heart attack. Not every warning sign is picked up on a stress test. And not every patient looks like the ones in the textbooks.

Sometimes, they look like me. Or like you.

CHAPTER 3 – The Rise (and Fall) of the Stress Test

Most people have heard of the stress test.

It's one of the most widely ordered heart tests in the world. Family doctors order it for peace of mind. Insurance companies use it as a screen. Pilots and executives are sent for one as part of their annual medicals. And many patients, especially those with risk factors, believe that if you "pass the stress test," you've passed the heart disease risk test.

I've seen it since the late nineties. Someone gets a stress test done, they get the all-clear, and they walk out with that magic phrase:

"Everything looks good."

But what does that really mean? I have seen and have heard of too many people passing a stress test, getting a clean bill of health from the cardiologist, only to have a heart attack weeks or months later.

This chapter is about how we got here, what the stress test does and doesn't do, and why it's no longer enough, especially if you're trying to prevent a heart attack or stroke.

The Origin of the Stress Test

The cardiac stress test was developed in the

1960s by Dr. Robert Bruce, the "father of exercise cardiology." He created what we now know as the Bruce Protocol: a treadmill-based test where patients walk at increasing speed and incline while their heart rhythm is monitored via ECG.

At the time, it was a breakthrough. It gave cardiologists a way to detect large-vessel coronary artery disease, the kind that causes significant obstruction and limits blood flow to the heart muscle during exercise.

And to be clear: it worked. For that purpose, in that era, it was a game-changer.

The problem? We've never really updated the thinking behind it.

We still use this test, essentially unchanged, to assess cardiovascular risk in people with no symptoms. Insurance companies give out million-dollar policies based on this archaic model. And in doing so, we miss the point entirely.

I Don't Hate Stress — I Hate the Outcomes

Let me be clear about one thing:

I love stress. I love what it does for performance, adaptation, and growth.

What I don't love, and what this chapter is about, are the two most common outcomes we've come to accept from stress testing. Because both are dangerously flawed.

Outcome #1: "You're Fine."

You go in. You walk the treadmill. You pass the test. You're told you're low risk.

But here's what most people, and many physicians don't realize: stress tests only detect advanced disease. You usually need a blockage of 70–80% before the ECG begins to show changes. That means you can have plaque, inflammation, instability, and walk away with a clean bill of health.

Up to 90% of heart attacks happen in people who "passed" their stress test.

Because what causes most heart attacks isn't a big, visible blockage. It's vulnerable plaque, small, inflamed lesions that rupture suddenly and block the artery with a clot.

That doesn't show up on a treadmill ECG.

Stress tests don't measure inflammation. They don't assess immune activity, endothelial function, or artery wall biology.

It's like checking the strength of a bridge by seeing how many trucks it can hold, without inspecting the cracks in the support beams.

The result?

A "normal" test. A false sense of security. And too often, a devastating event that "came out of nowhere."

CASE STUDY – The Runner

A 56-year-old patient came to us after recovering from a heart attack. He was a runner. Fit. Clean lifestyle. Two months before his event, his doctor had sent him for a stress test, just to be safe. He passed with flying colours. No symptoms. No flags.

He had a heart attack on a Saturday morning jog.

A stress test never would've caught his issue, because it wasn't about obstruction. It was about vulnerable plaque.

All I ask is that physicians take thirty seconds to say this:

"We performed a stress test, and it came out negative, which tells us you do not have advanced stages of heart disease. This test can still be wrong, so please pay attention to your lifestyle. Most heart attacks are not detected by this test."

So why did we do the test at all?

Because it's what's always been done. Because cardiology is still trained to look for clogged pipes, not unstable walls.

Outcome #2: "You've Got a Blockage."

Sometimes, the stress test flags electrical changes: ST segment changes, minor symptoms under exertion. And now you're on a path.

How to Read an ECG — The Quick and Dirty Guide

The electrocardiogram (ECG or EKG) is one of the first tools used when a patient presents with symptoms like chest pain, shortness of breath, or dizziness. It records the electrical activity of the heart and can offer a snapshot of your rhythm, rate, and sometimes signs of damage or strain.

Reading an ECG doesn't need to be intimidating. Here's the quick and dirty version:

- P wave: This small bump represents the contraction of the atria which are the upper chambers of the heart. If there's something off here, it may indicate atrial abnormalities like atrial enlargement or atrial fibrillation.
- QRS complex: This big spike reflects the contraction of the ventricles, the heart's main pumping chambers. It's the most dominant feature on the ECG and represents the actual heartbeat. Problems here may point to ventricular hypertrophy, conduction issues, or signs of ischemia (lack of blood flow).
- T wave: After the heart contracts, it needs to relax and reset. That's what the T wave shows. Abnormalities in the T wave can suggest relaxation issues (maybe time for a vacation:), electrolyte imbalances, or even early signs of a heart attack.

When someone arrives at the Emergency room with chest pain, the ECG is used first to check the rhythm and to look for signs of an active ST-elevation myocardial infarction (STEMI) a plaque rupture heart attack that needs emergency intervention. In this case, the ST segment between the QRS and T wave elevates, indicating a serious event.

But not all heart attacks show up on the ECG. Non-STEMI heart attacks often look normal on the tracing. That's why blood work (like troponin levels) is needed to confirm heart muscle damage. You'll want to make sure your care includes both ECG and labs in these cases.

And this brings us to stress testing. A stress ECG looks for ST segment changes under stress which is when the heart is working harder If the ST segment dips or elevates during exertion, it may suggest ischemia, or reduced blood flow to the heart muscle. This would then suggest advanced stages of disease. Does not mean you have to intervene with a heart stent or bypass.

Remember, these are all clues not definitive answers. Context is everything. I have seen too many times people getting a routine ECG, which most of the time is a waste of time.

Let's Investigate Further

So, if you "fail" the stress test, you're often sent down a rabbit hole:

A nuclear stress test

A CT angiogram

A cardiac catheterization (Angiogram)

Each one adds radiation, contrast dye, cost, and anxiety, often without improving clarity.

Sometimes, you're even offered a heart stent or bypass surgery, even though your disease is stable, your symptoms are mild, and better options exist.

CASE STUDY – The Over-Treated Executive

One of our patients was a 62-year-old executive. Mild fatigue. No pain. His stress test showed some mild ST depression. That led to a nuclear test, then a CT angiogram. The angiogram showed a 60% lesion in one artery. He was referred for a heart stent.

We reviewed his case and recommended a different path: optimal medical therapy, ECP, and lifestyle changes.

Six months later, he felt better than he had in years, without a single stent.

What Should Happen Instead: A Flowchart for Prevention

Here's how it should work, especially in non-emergency situations:

Symptoms?

- Yes → Rule out emergency (ECG, bloodwork)
- No → Go to next step

Risk Factors?

- Yes → Use biology-based testing
- No → Consider advanced markers only if high concern

Stress Test?

- Use only if symptoms or high suspicion of ischemia

Positive Test?

- Start with Optimal Medical Therapy
- Add Cardiac Rehab + Lifestyle Coaching
- Start External Counterpulsation Therapy (ECP) or structural imaging
- Reserve stents/surgery for failed medical therapy or unstable angina

This is what we do at Heart Fit Clinic, not because we're radical, but because it works.

What the Trials Actually Say

This isn't just my opinion. The evidence has been here for years, sitting in major peer-reviewed journals, funded by public institutions, designed to answer a question cardiology had been avoiding for too long:

Are we over-treating stable patients?

That question didn't come out of nowhere. It came from decades of watching interventional cardiology expand, not just in emergencies (where it saves lives), but into the gray zone of stable, asymptomatic patients. Patients who were being sent to the cath lab simply because of a stress test result. The assumption was always the same: if there's a blockage, open it. If it looks tight, fix it. Whether the patient was in pain or not.

Stents became routine, and profitable.

Hospitals built cath labs. Cardiologists sharpened their technique. Patients walked away believing they'd "fixed" their heart disease because someone placed a stent. But the field never really asked the harder follow-up questions:

Does this change outcomes for stable patients?

Does it actually save lives? And what else are we exposing them to in the process?

Because the truth is, with every stent, even in a stable patient, comes not just the procedure itself, but the automatic addition of dual antiplatelet therapy. Blood thinners that carry their own risks: bruising, gastrointestinal bleeding, and in some cases, serious hemorrhage. And if the stent wasn't necessary in the first place, then neither were the drugs that followed.

That's why these trials were born, to ask the hard questions, not just about procedures, but about the entire treatment cascade that follows them.

The COURAGE Trial (2007) was one of the first major wake-up calls. It compared optimal medical therapy, medication, risk factor control, lifestyle, to stenting in patients with stable coronary artery disease. And the results were a shock to many: stenting did not reduce the risk of heart attack or death. Over several years of follow-up, patients who managed their disease with medications and lifestyle fared just as well as those who had invasive procedures.

It didn't say stents had no role. It said they weren't necessary in stable disease if symptoms were manageable and risk factors were under control.

Then came the ORBITA Trial (2017), a bold and controversial study that raised eyebrows across the field. This was a sham-controlled trial, patients were randomized to receive either a real stent or a fake procedure. Neither the patients nor the physicians knew who received what.

The question was simple: does placing a stent actually improve symptoms, or do we just believe it does?

The answer: there was no significant difference in exercise time or angina relief between the stent and placebo groups. Much of the perceived benefit, it turned out, may have been the placebo effect.

ORBITA didn't sit well with everyone, especially those who had spent years equating intervention with benefit. But it reinforced what COURAGE had already hinted at: we're doing a lot of procedures that don't change the outcome, and may trigger unnecessary follow-up treatments.

Then came the ISCHEMIA Trial (2020), which took things further. It studied more than 5,000 patients with moderate to severe ischemia, the kind of result that almost always leads to angiography and often to stents or surgery. But this trial asked: what if we held off and started with medical therapy first?

Once again, the results held: no difference in

death, heart attack, or hospitalization over several years. Invasive treatment helped with symptoms, yes, particularly in patients with frequent angina. But it didn't prevent heart attacks. It didn't save lives.

And yet here we are, years later, and we are still sending stable, asymptomatic patients down a diagnostic and procedural pathway. Still implanting devices that don't extend life. Still adding blood thinners that increase bleeding risk. Still calling it "prevention" when in many cases, it's just reaction, dressed up with imaging and intervention.

These weren't fringe studies. They were meticulously designed, independently funded, and led by some of the world's most respected cardiovascular researchers. They weren't about denying care. They were about redefining appropriate care.

And they've been telling us the same thing again and again:

Yes, we are doing too much. Especially when we ignore what lifestyle, cardiac rehabilitation, and optimal medical therapy can do.

So the question is no longer: "Should we rethink stress testing?"

The question is: "Why haven't we?"

Why the Stress Test Persists (and Why the System Doesn't Change)

Let me be fair.

I have tremendous respect for cardiologists. They are trained to respond to emergencies, and they do it exceptionally well. In an acute setting, an active heart attack, unstable angina, rhythm disturbances, you want a cardiologist by your side.

But cardiology is still built around crisis response, not prevention.

As I heard at the Canadian Cardiovascular Congress:
"Cardiologists are trained to not tolerate ischemia."

That makes sense in the ER. It does not make sense in the outpatient setting, where patients have stable symptoms, or no symptoms at all.

We can't wait for institutions to change from the inside. The system is designed for throughput, not long consultations, not root-cause investigation.

I'm not here to fight cardiology. I'm here to support patients.

Let the evidence speak for itself.

A Better Way to Assess Risk

If you want to truly prevent heart disease, look beyond the stress test.

Instead of focusing only on blockages, assess:

Endothelial function

Inflammation and immune activity

Artery wall thickness and vulnerability

Lipoprotein particle size

Microvascular function and autonomic balance

This is what we do at Heart Fit Clinic, because it works.

This isn't alternative. This is science-based, patient-centered medicine. It's prevention, not reaction.

What Comes Next

The problem isn't the stress test itself. It's how we interpret it. It's what we do with it. And most of all, it's what we fail to see when we rely on it too much.

To understand why that's so dangerous, we have to go deeper. Because arteries aren't pipes.

They're muscles. They're living tissue. And that's what we'll explore next.

CHAPTER 4 – What Are We Really Testing?

So, you might have had a cardiac test before and are now wondering whether it was the right thing, or may even be wondering what we should do next.

Maybe you've had an ECG. Maybe a stress test. Maybe your doctor ordered a CT angiogram or sent you for a calcium score. Maybe you've had a nuclear scan. Maybe you've even had a heart stent or bypass surgery.

The assumption is always the same:

"If I've had the right test, I'll know where I stand."

But here's the truth:

You can have all the tests… and still miss the problem entirely.

Why? Because most heart tests aren't designed to detect early or unstable disease. These "hidden" blockages are the kind that causes heart attacks. They're good at identifying blockages that are already severe, or damage that's already been done. But they're terrible at predicting risk before the crisis.

In this chapter, we're going to break that down. I'll walk you through the three systems of the heart, the tests most commonly used in each one, and what they do, what they don't, and determine what they actually tell you.

The Heart Has Three Systems

To understand testing, you first need to understand what you're testing for. Most people along with many physicians, still see the heart as a single system: a pump with pipes.

But your heart functions across three major systems:

System	What It Involves	Examples
Electrical	Heart rhythm and signal conduction	Atrial fibrillation, tachycardia
Structural	Valve function, chamber size, pumping	Valve disease, heart failure
Plumbing	Blood flow through coronary arteries	Atherosclerosis, ischemia

Different problems show up in different systems. And different tests look at different systems. That's why a normal test in one system doesn't mean your heart is healthy overall.

Think of the heart like a house. You have the structure of the house. You have the electricity of the house. And then you have the plumbing. But as you may or may not know, these arteries are not a pipe. They are a muscle. There is a lot of biology to them.

The Tests Most People Get — and What They Really Show

Electrical Testing (Rhythm)

These tests tell us about your heart's electrical wiring.- how it fires, how it resets, and whether it's in rhythm.

ECG (Electrocardiogram) – A snapshot of your rhythm in the moment. Can detect arrhythmias, previous heart damage, or signs of acute heart attack (but only if it's happening right now).

Holter Monitor – Worn for at least 24–72 hours to capture intermittent rhythm problems like atrial fibrillation or PVCs.

Event Monitor / Patch – Longer-term monitoring, up to 14 days or more.

Electrophysiology Study – An invasive procedure to map electrical pathways before an ablation.

Electrophysiology Study (EPS) & Ablation

An electrophysiology study (EPS) is an invasive test used to evaluate the electrical activity of the heart. It's performed in a hospital or specialized EP (electrophysiology) lab by a cardiac electrophysiologist, a cardiologist who specializes in heart rhythm disorders.

EPS is typically ordered when standard ECGs or Holter monitors haven't explained symptoms like palpitations or fainting. There's concern for life-threatening arrhythmias such as ventricular tachycardia or atrial fibrillation. Or a patient is being evaluated for catheter ablation, a pacemaker, or an implantable cardioverter defibrillator (ICD).

What happens during the test is that one or more catheters are inserted through a vein in the groin, neck, or arm. These are guided into the heart using live X-ray imaging (fluoroscopy). Electrodes on the catheter tips record the electrical activity from inside the heart. The heart may be stimulated with small electrical impulses to provoke an arrhythmia in a safe, controlled setting. This allows the physician to map the heart's electrical system in real time and locate the source of any abnormal rhythms.

The EPS typically takes one to two hours. If ablation is performed in the same session, total time may extend to three to four hours. The procedure uses fluoroscopy, which exposes the patient to radiation, often between 5–15 millisieverts (mSv), depending on procedure length and complexity (roughly the equivalent of 250–750 chest X-rays).

Catheter Ablation: Treating the Problem at Its Source

If an abnormal rhythm is identified, the same procedure can often move directly into catheter ablation. Using the same catheter, the physician applies energy, typically radiofrequency (heat) or cryoablation (cold), to carefully destroy the small area of heart tissue causing the arrhythmia.

Ablation is most commonly used to treat: atrial fibrillation (AFib), supraventricular tachycardia (SVT), atrial flutter, and certain cases of ventricular tachycardia.

The goal is to interrupt the faulty electrical circuit, restore normal rhythm, and reduce or eliminate the need for medications. In many patients, catheter ablation is life-changing which may dramatically improve symptoms and quality of life.

But it's important to be clear: EPS and ablation are not tests for coronary artery disease. They do not assess blockages or plaque, inflammation of the artery wall, or risk of heart attack or stroke.

They are rhythm tools, not vascular tools. If you're concerned about heart disease risk, this is not the test you need.

When EPS Makes Sense — and When It Doesn't

EPS is invaluable when the issue is electrical, especially when other tests haven't explained symptoms or when there's a known arrhythmia. But it's not useful as a screening tool, and it's not appropriate for general heart health assessment.

If you're dizzy, fainting, skipping beats, or

feeling heart flutters, the EPS might be your test. But if you're worried about a heart attack or your arteries? This test won't get you closer to that answer.

Structural Testing (Valves and Muscle Function)

These evaluate how your heart is built and how well it pumps blood.

Echocardiogram – An ultrasound of the heart. Shows valve function, wall motion, ejection fraction.

Transesophageal Echocardiogram (TEE) – A high-resolution echo done from the esophagus to get better images of the valves.

Cardiac MRI – Provides detailed views of heart structure, muscle damage, and scarring.

LV Function Tests – Used in heart failure patients to determine treatment eligibility (e.g., for LVAD or transplant).

What they miss: These tests don't evaluate artery health or detect early coronary disease. You can have a perfect echo and still be at high risk of a heart attack.

Plumbing Testing (Blood Flow and Blockages)

This is where most people get tested, and where the biggest blind spots exist.

We've been told for decades that cholesterol is the villain in the heart disease story. But what if it's just a character, and not the main plot?

Books like The Great Cholesterol Myth by Dr. Jonny Bowden and Dr. Stephen Sinatra have helped bring this debate to light, supported by cardiologists like Dr. Jack Wolfson, who argue that focusing narrowly on cholesterol has distracted us from the real causes: inflammation, oxidative stress, insulin resistance, and endothelial dysfunction.

Dr. Wolfson, a board-certified cardiologist turned integrative practitioner, says it clearly:

"Statins lower a number, not your real risk. And they can do more harm than good when prescribed broadly without looking at the whole patient."

Even the literature agrees. Meta-analyses on statin use for primary prevention who are people who haven't had a heart attack, show modest benefits at best, with no meaningful difference in all-cause mortality for low-risk populations.

Lowering LDL to impress a guideline doesn't necessarily lower your actual danger of a heart event, especially if inflammation, blood sugar, and artery wall integrity are ignored.

That's why so many of the patients in hospital with a heart attack don't have high cholesterol. And it's why some people with "perfect" LDL numbers still drop dead unexpectedly.

Cholesterol plays a role but it's not the root. And treating a symptom is not the same as treating the cause.

Cholesterol Testing — And the Story We've Been Sold

We've been talking about cholesterol for decades, but not always accurately.

The idea that cholesterol "clogs arteries" can be traced back to the 1970s, when researchers opened up cadaver arteries and found two things in the plaque: cholesterol and fat. At the time, it made sense to blame those components for the buildup. It was simple, visual, and easy to understand that cholesterol was the gunk in the pipes.

Not long after, pharmaceutical companies began developing drugs that could lower LDL cholesterol. When statins were finally introduced and proven to reduce LDL, the entire public health machine jumped on board. Media headlines followed suit. Macleans, Time, and other major publications splashed provocative covers across newsstands: "Cholesterol: The Silent Killer" and "Fighting the Clog" became common themes.

That was the birth of the cholesterol panic.

Soon, cholesterol wasn't just seen as a marker, it was the villain. Dietary fat became the enemy. Eggs, butter, red meat all were demonized. "Low-fat" and "fat-free" labels flooded supermarket shelves. Cholesterol-free became a marketing badge of honor.

But here's what happened next:

As we removed fat and cholesterol from our

diets, we replaced them with processed carbohydrates, added sugars, and industrial oils. Rates of diabetes, obesity, and metabolic dysfunction exploded along with the burden of heart disease. We didn't solve the problem. We shifted it.

And we never stopped to ask: Was cholesterol ever the root cause?

Today, we know cholesterol isn't that simple. When we test it, we're looking at broad categories: LDL, often labeled the "bad" cholesterol; HDL, the "good"; and triglycerides, the "ugly." But this framework is outdated. Not all LDL is dangerous. Not all HDL is protective. And total cholesterol alone is almost meaningless.

What matters far more is how that cholesterol behaves in the body, its particle size, oxidation state, and how your artery wall responds to it.

We've known this for years. The landmark Get With The Guidelines (GWTG) study reviewed over 136,000 patients hospitalized with coronary artery disease. Nearly 75% of them had LDL levels below 130 mg/dL (3.4 mmol/L), and almost 50% were below 100 mg/dL (2.6 mmol/L).

In other words, the majority of people who had heart attacks did not have high cholesterol.

That's not a fluke. That's a flaw in the model.

You can have "normal" LDL and still have plaque that is inflamed, unstable, and ready to rupture. You can be in the "safe zone" on paper and still be vulnerable to a major event.

The standard lipid panel won't tell you that. It doesn't measure endothelial health. It doesn't assess plaque activity. It doesn't look at the biology of the artery wall.

This is why traditional cholesterol testing is no longer enough, because the real risk isn't just how much cholesterol you have. It's how it behaves. It's how your body handles it. Most importantly, it's what happens at the artery wall that determines your true risk.

Statins, Marketing, and the Truth About Risk

It's hard to talk about cholesterol without talking about statins, and even harder without talking about how they've been marketed.

For decades now, statins have been positioned as the ultimate weapon against heart disease. If your cholesterol is high, take a statin. If your cholesterol is borderline, take a statin. If you've had a heart event, of course, take a statin. It's almost reflexive. But have we really understood what they're doing, and what they're not?

You've probably seen an ad like the one with Dr. Robert Jarvik, inventor of the Jarvik Artificial Heart, standing next to a glowing animation of an artery. The ad proclaims in big, bold numbers: "Lipitor reduces risk of heart attack by 36%."

Sounds impressive. Sounds like a no-brainer.

But read the small print, and the truth tells a different story.

What that 36% refers to is relative risk reduction. In the clinical trial, 3% of patients on a sugar pill had a heart attack, compared to 2% of those taking Lipitor. That's an absolute difference of just 1%, but because 2 is 36% less than 3, that's the number they ran with.

This is a classic case of relative vs. absolute risk, and unless you read carefully, it's easy to be misled.

The more meaningful measure is called the Number Needed to Treat (NNT). This tells us how many people need to take a drug for one person to benefit. In the Lipitor trial, the NNT was 100, meaning 100 people had to take the drug for five years to prevent one heart attack. The other 99 saw no benefit at all.

And that's in high-risk individuals. In lower-risk populations, the NNT rises even higher, sometimes over 250. That's 250 people taking a daily medication (often with side effects) so that one person may avoid a nonfatal event.

Even in newer statin-adjacent trials, like the FOURIER trial, which studied a powerful LDL-lowering injectable drug (evolocumab), we see a familiar pattern. Yes, it lowered LDL by 74%, which sounds spectacular. But the actual absolute risk reduction in hard endpoints (like death, heart attack, stroke) was around 1.5% over 2.2 years. That's an NNT of about 67 — again, underwhelming when you consider the hype and cost.

None of this is to say statins are useless. In secondary prevention, meaning people who've already had a heart attack or stent, statins do play a role. They reduce recurrent events. But even there, the benefit is modest, and the risks (muscle pain, fatigue, brain fog, elevated blood sugar) aren't always discussed.

The bigger issue is that we've built a treatment model focused on lowering numbers, not understanding why the risk exists in the first place.

Cholesterol isn't the villain. It's a passenger in a much more complex story, one involving inflammation, oxidation, immune response, endothelial dysfunction, and arterial biology.

This is why so many patients with "perfect" cholesterol still have heart attacks. It's why statins often disappoint in primary prevention. And it's why blindly chasing lower LDL while ignoring the root causes, won't lead to better outcomes.

If we're going to prescribe medications that half the population over 50 is expected to take for life, we need to be honest about what they do... and what they don't.

Stress Test (Treadmill ECG)

The treadmill ECG stress test evaluates how your heart responds to exercise, specifically looking for electrical changes that suggest reduced blood flow to the heart muscle (ischemia).

Here's how it works:

As you walk on a treadmill, your heart rate and blood pressure increase. Electrodes record your heart's electrical activity. The test looks for ST segment changes on the ECG, patterns that may indicate reduced oxygen reaching the heart muscle during stress.

That might sound useful, but here's the problem:

You usually need a blockage of 70% or more in a major artery to produce these changes. But the majority of heart attacks occur at sites of less than 50% blockage.

These are the hidden dangers, vulnerable plaques that are inflamed, unstable, and ready to rupture, but not large enough to restrict blood flow during a treadmill test. With a sensitivity of ~60–70%, and a specificity: ~70–80%, a stress test misses the vast majority of early-stage or vulnerable plaques but also means it can miss heart disease even when present.

Even the American Heart Association acknowledges: a "negative" stress test does not mean you're free of coronary artery disease.

Why This Matters

Let's say you have early plaque, inflamed, active, but not yet obstructive. You take the test. You pass. You walk away thinking, "I'm fine."

But your body is still a ticking time bomb,

and no one told you that this test couldn't catch it.

Nuclear Stress Test (Also known as Thallium, MIBI, Sestamibi, Myocardial Perfusion Imaging)

The nuclear stress test is one of the most commonly ordered second-line tests, especially after an inconclusive or mildly abnormal treadmill ECG.

It works like this:

You're injected with a radioactive tracer, usually Thallium or Technetium (Sestamibi). You exercise (or are given a drug to simulate exercise). A gamma camera takes images of your heart, before and after stress, to evaluate blood flow (perfusion) to the heart muscle.

If certain areas of the heart receive less tracer during stress, and then refill normally at rest, it suggests reversible ischemia.

The Problem

This test isn't subtle. The nuclear stress test is designed to detect large, flow-limiting blockages, not early disease, not inflamed plaque, and certainly not the kind of instability that leads to most heart attacks. It tells you how blood moves through the arteries under stress, but it tells you nothing about whether your artery wall is quiet or dangerous, stable or about to rupture. And on top of that, it comes with a dose of radiation that's far more significant than most people realize.

A typical nuclear stress test exposes the body to somewhere between 500 and 750 chest X-rays worth of radiation, around 10 to 15 millisieverts (mSv). For perspective, a basic chest X-ray is about 0.02 mSv. A mammogram is 0.4 mSv. A full-body CT scan sits around 10 mSv. The nuclear stress test matches or exceeds that. And that's not even accounting for the radioactive tracer, which stays in your body for hours, sometimes days, and may have long-term effects on DNA, especially with repeated exposure.

So, the question becomes: Was that test necessary?
Or was it just protocol?

Overuse and False Security

Many nuclear tests are ordered not because of active concern, but because someone failed a basic stress test, or because "this is just what we do."

The problem is that this test often leads to false positives, followed by invasive procedures that may not improve long-term outcomes. And when the test is "normal," it gives false reassurance, because again, early disease goes undetected.

It tells us how blood moves. But it tells us nothing about why you're at risk.

It doesn't assess the artery health and biology. In other words: it doesn't see the real cause of most heart attacks.

Like the standard treadmill stress test, nuclear stress tests have real limitations when it comes to identifying meaningful, actionable risk. The

Sensitivity: ~80–85%, which is where it correctly detects disease in ~80–85% of people who have significant obstructive CAD. Specificity: ~70–75%, which is when it correctly identifies those who don't have disease)

That may sound decent, until you remember what it's measuring: only large, flow-limiting blockages, not early disease, inflammation, or plaque rupture potential.

Worse, in real-world clinical use (especially among low-to-intermediate-risk populations), these numbers drop significantly, leading to false positives, unnecessary invasive procedures, and even overtreatment.

Most people undergoing a nuclear stress test don't end up with a procedure that changes their outcome. But they do walk away exposed to radiation, and often, a misbelief that they're "in the clear."

CT Coronary Angiography (or CTA)

This test is often positioned as a less invasive alternative to a traditional angiogram. Therefore, overused for people who want to know the plumbing of the heart when they are stable. It's used to create a 3D image of the coronary arteries using contrast dye and high-dose radiation. On paper, it sounds like the ideal tool to catch coronary disease before it becomes a problem.

But it's not that simple.

What It Actually Shows

The CT angiogram gives us a picture, which is a still image of the larger coronary arteries. It can identify visible plaque buildup, significant blockages along with overall anatomy of major coronary vessels.

It's a good tool when you need to rule out severe obstruction. But that's all it does. It doesn't show inflammation, vulnerability, or unstable plaque as well. In fact, it can't, because of what it can and cannot see.

The Real Limitation: Resolution

The average main coronary artery is about 300 micrometers in diameter. That's roughly the diameter of a quarter or a Canadian loonie.

CT imaging can just barely resolve that. But what about the branching vessels, or the microvascular arteries, which can be as small as 30 micrometers (human hair) or much less (under 10 microns), not even visible to the naked eye?

Those arteries, invisible to the CT scan, are often where early dysfunction begins.

You could have inflammation, endothelial dysfunction, or microvascular ischemia, and a CT angiogram will miss it completely.

That's a dangerous blind spot.

Radiation and Contrast Dye Exposure

To get this image, the patient must receive:

Iodinated contrast dye, which is filtered through the kidneys and can be harmful to those with kidney disease or diabetes. High-dose radiation, often in the range of 5–10 millisieverts (mSv), the equivalent of 250–500 chest X-rays

And unlike the nuclear stress test, CT radiation is delivered all at once, making it a higher biological impact.

Now consider this: you're exposing the body to that kind of stress to detect a plaque big enough to be seen, rather than assessing the real reasons that plaque becomes dangerous.

The Sensitivity: ~85–90% for detecting obstructive coronary artery disease in the proximal segments. And the specificity: ~65–75%, meaning false positives are common, especially in people with calcium in their arteries. It doesn't detect the early, unstable, or inflammatory stages of heart disease that lead to most heart attacks.

CASE STUDY: When a CT Angiogram Gets It Wrong

One patient Mrs. V came to me after a CT coronary angiogram suggested severe coronary artery disease. The CT report described:

Severe narrowing at the origin of the left anterior descending (LAD) artery.

A possible blockage in the distal right coronary artery (RCA).

Multiple calcified plaques.

A "filling defect" that could be a soft plaque or even a thrombus.

The language in the report was alarming and it put the patient in a high short-to-medium-term cardiac risk group. Naturally, this triggered a referral for an invasive coronary angiogram.

The Reality Check

Just four days later, the invasive angiogram, the so-called "gold standard", told a very different story:

Left main artery: normal.

LAD: only a 20% narrowing in the proximal segment which was far from obstructive.

Circumflex and RCA: completely normal.

Final conclusion: Non-obstructive coronary artery disease.

No stent. No bypass. No emergency.

Why the CT Got It Wrong?

CT angiograms are prone to false positives, especially in people with significant calcification. Calcium "blooms" on the image, making the artery look narrower than it really is. Add in motion artifacts, limitations in resolution, and interpretive bias (once a high calcium score is seen, the mind starts looking for trouble), and you can turn a stable patient into an "urgent case" on paper.

What was the Cost of Overcalling Disease?

In this case, the CT scan's overestimation led to an unnecessary invasive procedure, with its own risks and costs. Significant anxiety for the patient along with a detour from addressing the actual drivers of heart attack risk which is the biology, inflammation, and lifestyle. Now let's be clear, she has artery disease but not an obstruction. This is where even if there was a heart stent or bypass surgery was not going to save her no matter what the conclusion of the angiogram, because she was not having an active heart attack.

CT angiograms can be valuable when they're clean, a normal test can spare someone from unnecessary testing. But when calcium is present, interpretation becomes tricky, and false alarms are common. That's why test results should always be interpreted in the context of symptoms, risk profile, along when appropriate and functional or physiological testing before committing someone to the cath lab.

Coronary Artery Calcium (CAC)

This is a scoring is often marketed as a quick, affordable, low-radiation screening test for heart disease. It's a CT scan of the chest that measures the amount of calcium in your coronary arteries.

Calcium is a sign of plaque. So, the idea is simple:

Higher score = more plaque = more risk

Zero score = no plaque = no risk

53

But it's not that simple.

What the Test Actually Shows

The CAC score only detects calcified plaque, not soft plaque, not inflamed plaque, not unstable or vulnerable plaque.

But the plaques most likely to rupture and cause a heart attack are often soft and non-calcified.

In fact, most heart attacks occur where there is no visible calcium.

The score doesn't detect:

Inflammation, Endothelial dysfunction, Early atherosclerosis, Plaque composition or vulnerability.

So, if all you see is a "0" calcium score, you're missing the full picture.

Real-World Patient Example

I had a patient who received a "zero" calcium score from a routine scan. Their cardiologist said, "You're good to go." But, they did not feel great.

But they pushed for more answers. They did a CT angiogram, and it showed a moderate blockage made of non-calcified plaque.

Had he stopped at the calcium score, he'd be walking around thinking he was bulletproof. And yet, he was walking around with a vulnerable, dangerous lesion.

On the other end, I've had patients with calcium scores over 1,000 even over 2,000, with no symptoms, no events, and decades of good health. Because calcified plaque can often mean stable disease, a scar of the past, not necessarily a warning of the future. This is why it is important to look at the full biology of the artery.

Sensitivity, Specificity, and Radiation

Sensitivity: Very high for detecting calcified plaque, but poor for non-calcified or soft plaque.

Specificity: Moderate, can't distinguish between stable and unstable plaque.

Radiation dose: ~1–3 mSv (about 50–150 chest X-rays)

It's relatively low-risk compared to a nuclear test or CTA. But the risk is not in the scan, it's in the false confidence that can follow.

Invasive Coronary Angiogram (Cardiac Catheterization)

This is often called the gold standard in cardiology, with a sensitivity of 90–95% for detecting significant (>70%) blockages in large vessels and specificity of 95%+, very accurate for showing what's there.

The invasive coronary angiogram is a procedure performed in the Cath lab. It involves:

Inserting a catheter through the femoral artery (groin) or radial artery (wrist). Threading it up through the aorta to reach the coronary arteries (this can hurt the endothelial lining of the artery). Then injecting iodinated contrast dye while taking real-time X-ray images (fluoroscopy) of the coronary vessels.

This allows cardiologists to see the inside of the artery lumen and identify any narrowing or blockages.

When It's Lifesaving

Make no mistake, this test can save lives. If someone is having a heart attack, experiencing unstable angina, or showing clear signs of acute coronary syndrome

Then an invasive angiogram is the fastest, most definitive way to: Identify the culprit lesion, open it with a stent or bypass surgery, and restore blood flow and save the heart muscle

In those moments, you want a cath lab. And you want an interventional cardiologist at the helm.

But what about someone who's stable?

Someone with mild symptoms… or someone who simply failed a stress test?

That's where things go off the rails.

Too often, patients are sent straight to the cath lab not because they need it, but because the protocol says so.

But if you're not having an emergency, an invasive angiogram:

Doesn't improve long-term outcomes

Doesn't reduce your risk of future heart attack

And may not lead to a procedure at all

In these cases, a CT angiogram might be an option, or cardiac rehabilitation, External Counterpulsation and at least starting optimal medical therapy would be better along with looking at the artery biology would be very beneficial

The Invasive Angiogram on its own does not look at plaque activity, unless we do intravascular ultrasound, or optimal coherence tomography which is more radiation exposure and damage to the endothelium. There are cases where it is valuable for stent insertion. It does miss endothelial dysfunction, early disease in arteries not yet obstructed, microvascular or branch-level disease. Many times, especially women or diabetics, can have ischemia or myocardial infarction with non-obstructive coronary arteries (INOCA / MINOCA).

MINOCA sounds like a great camera, but I remember when I started many times people went the cath lab with heart attack or symptoms and told it was in their head. Many times, these patients were diabetic or women. But they were told to go home that the pain must be something else. It was not until a lot more women who came into cardiology researched more into this. As many women were experiencing symptoms and told it was in their head. Now heart attacks don't lie, with troponins and cardiac enzymes that were elevated along with possible ECG changes. The protocol was correct to send them to the cath lab for an angiogram, but found that the major coronaries were normal. This is what precipitated the research and now there are some good functional angiogram testing available to see how and what the arteries do under duress. Again, I love what External Counterpulsation does for these patients, with MINOCA, INOCA, and microvascular disease. In fact, I love it for all artery disease.

Radiation and Contrast Risk

Radiation: 5 to 10 mSv (about 250 to500 chest X-rays). Contrast dye: Risk of nephropathy (kidney injury), especially in diabetics or people with impaired kidney function. Bleeding, hematoma, arrhythmia, vascular damage, rare, but real procedural risks.

And remember: this test is invasive. It's not a screening tool. It's not for peace of mind. It's a procedure, with real physical cost.

An invasive coronary angiogram is the right tool when there's clear, immediate concern for obstructive, unstable coronary disease.

But it's not prevention. It's not a risk test. And it's not the end of the story, even if the images look "good."

Just because the pipe looks clean, doesn't mean the wall isn't compromised.

There is more that you can do.

In Summary:

What they miss: Almost all of these tests evaluate plumbing from the inside out, but heart attacks don't start with big blockages. They start with a biology concern, none of which show up on these tests.

The reality is this: Most tests were designed to detect late-stage disease. They weren't built for prevention. They were built to confirm a diagnosis after a patient already has symptoms.

But in the majority of fatal heart attacks, the first symptom is the heart attack itself.

So, by the time the system "catches it," it's too late. That's not a failure of the test. It's a failure of the model. If you've already had a heart event, certain tests are absolutely necessary.

But if you're trying to avoid one, or if you've been told "you're fine" based on a stress test or cholesterol panel, it's time to go deeper.

You don't need more testing. You need smarter testing.

Because if you're looking for the wrong thing, you'll never know what you've missed.

What is smarter testing?

If we truly want to prevent heart attacks, not just react to them, we need to go beyond looking for visible blockages.

Instead, we should be asking:

How healthy are the arteries?

How well are they functioning?

What's happening at the biological level, beneath the surface?

That's where real prevention starts, not with how opened my arteries are, but with artery health, function, and biology.

This means moving beyond traditional imaging and standard cholesterol panels and instead focusing on: How arteries respond, what inflammatory processes are active and whether the vessel wall is vulnerable or stable.

There are modern tools that assess these factors. They're non-invasive. They don't involve radiation. And they're built for what matters most: early detection and prevention, not just emergency response.

If you want to know whether you're heading toward a heart event, not just whether you already had one, these are the kinds of questions to ask.

CHAPTER 5 – Arteries Are a Muscle, Not a Pipe

We've been taught to think of arteries like pipes.

I remember early in my career, working with the cardiology group at Total Cardiology in Calgary. It was one of the most respected teams in the city, and I was lucky to be learning from them. But one thing was repeated so often, so consistently, it became gospel:

"It's a plumbing problem."

Arteries were pipes. If they were clogged, you cleared them. If they were blocked, you opened them up. It was ingrained into our heads, this idea that heart disease was just a matter of fixing flow. I can still hear it echoing in case discussions and cath lab debriefs: "Let's snake the pipes. Let's stent the narrowing. Let's bypass the blockage."

Clogged pipes. Narrow pipes. Blocked pipes.

If something went wrong, it is treated it like a mechanical issue. Open up the artery and we improved the flow. We fixed the plumbing. Now this is very important if you are having a heart attack. But the same model was being applied to even if you did not have a heart attack.

That model has been baked into the public narrative for decades, reinforced by cartoons, commercials, and even well-meaning doctors who are simply repeating what they were taught.

But over time, I began to see something that didn't fit.

People with clean or partially blocked arteries were still having heart attacks. People with major blockages were living full, symptom-free lives. Some with perfect cholesterol were collapsing. Others with multiple stents were still declining.

Something didn't add up.

And that's when I started to ask:

What if arteries aren't pipes at all?

What if they're something more complex, more intelligent, more alive?

Here's the truth:

Your arteries are not pipes.

Pipes are passive. They just carry stuff. But your arteries are living, dynamic, reactive tissue. They expand. They contract. They respond to stress. They respond to oxygen demand. They respond to inflammation.

They're not plumbing.

They're muscle.

And muscle can adapt. Muscle can heal.

Muscle can change.

That's what this chapter is about.

Because when you stop thinking about arteries as tubes and start thinking of them as tissue, as responsive, living muscle, you open the door to a completely different understanding of how heart disease works... and how to truly prevent it. Let's dive in to anatomy 101 to the artery wall.

The Endothelium — The Forgotten Organ

Lining every artery in your body is a thin, complex layer called the endothelium. It's only one cell thick, but it controls everything from blood flow to inflammation to clotting.

In fact, the endothelium is now considered the largest organ in the body when laid out end to end, stretching over 60,000 miles of blood vessels.

The endothelium isn't just a lining. It's an active, intelligent surface.

It senses pressure, oxygen demand, stress hormones, nitric oxide, and toxins.

It opens or tightens the artery in response.

It decides whether cholesterol sticks or slides off.

It calls in the immune system, or tells it to stand down.

When the endothelium is healthy, it protects you.

When it's inflamed, it becomes a danger zone.

This is where heart disease begins, not as a blockage, but as a wound on the inside of a living system.

The Glycocalyx — The First Line of Defense

Coating the endothelium, the inner lining of every artery, is an even more delicate structure called the glycocalyx.

Think of it as the "skin on the skin" a hair-like, gel-like layer that acts as a protective barrier between your blood and the vessel wall.

The glycocalyx has several critical functions:

It repels harmful particles like small cholesterol particles and toxins.

It helps sense shear stress (blood flow) and regulates nitric oxide release

It prevents platelets and inflammatory cells from sticking to the endothelium

It helps maintain smooth, frictionless blood flow

When the glycocalyx is intact, it's like a shield, a natural anti-inflammatory, anti-clotting, and anti-atherosclerotic surface.

But when it's damaged; by high blood sugar, oxidative stress, inflammation, environmental exposures or tobacco smoke, the defenses are down.

And when the glycocalyx breaks down, the endothelium is left exposed, vulnerable, sticky, and primed for injury. The damage doesn't happen because the surface is defective, it happens because it lost its protection.

I remember taking my boys fishing on the coast of Puerto Vallarta. We'd caught a few fish and were bringing them in. You can smell the fresh ocean water, and yes when you catch the fish you either love or hate that smell. One of my sons reached down to pick one up, fresh from the ocean, and it slipped right through his hands. We all laughed as it flopped across the deck. That fish was nearly impossible to grip because of a slick, slippery coating on its surface, a protective layer that nature built to keep it healthy in the water.

But later, when it came time to clean the fish, the ones we hadn't frozen yet, it was a different story. They were easier to handle. That slick layer had started to wear off. The fish felt dry, sticky, and vulnerable. That coating, which once made it untouchable, was gone.

Your glycocalyx works the same way. When it's intact, it acts as a barrier, preventing harmful substances from sticking to the artery wall. But once it's damaged, from high blood sugar, oxidative stress, toxins, or inflammation, the endothelium underneath becomes exposed and reactive. That's when cholesterol can sliver in the lining, and that Is when immune cells show up and stick to the lining of the endothelium. That's when heart disease starts, not with a blockage, but with a wound on the artery wall.

This is part of the foundation for improving your artery health.

The Sub-endothelium — Where Plaque Lives

Beneath the endothelial surface is the subendothelial space, a layer where cholesterol and immune cells accumulate if damage occurs.

This is where vulnerable plaque begins to form. And it's this plaque, not a giant blockage, that suddenly ruptures, clots, and causes heart attacks or strokes.

Here's the key:

It's not the size of the plaque. It's the biology of the plaque.

Most heart attacks happen in mild-to-moderate lesions that never show up on standard tests, but are unstable, inflamed, and active.

Artery Function vs. Artery Anatomy

Modern cardiology is still focused on anatomy:

How blocked is the pipe?

But what we should be asking is:

How well is the artery functioning? How does it respond under stress? Is the wall inflamed? Is the plaque stable or vulnerable?

This shift from plumbing to biology changes

everything.

And it changes what we test for.

Arteries Can Heal

This is the good news.

Because arteries are muscle, not fixed metal tubes, they can change. They can regenerate. They can form new pathways (collaterals). They can reverse inflammation. They can even stabilize or shrink plaque.

But that only happens if we treat the biology, not just the blockage. People always ask how can we unclog our arteries, and my answer is they are not a pipe they are a muscle. You can feel these arteries expand and contract especially the ones close to the surface of our skin (neck, wrist, ankles). There is a lot of biology that happens to these muscles and there are unique reasons why people undergo these biology concerns

You don't fix this by stenting a spot on the map or scraping out the plaque.

You fix this by:

Lowering inflammation

Improving endothelial function

Restoring nitric oxide pathways

Modifying immune system response

Supporting metabolic health

And that means you need different tools, different tests, and a different conversation with your doctor that they may not be used to yet.

The Old Model Is Breaking

You can hear it behind the scenes.

In conferences. In back rooms. In frustrated conversations between progressive cardiologists and rigid institutions. The truth is, the plumbing model no longer fits the science. We've just been slow to admit it publicly. Cardiologist are trained for emergent situations but to prevent emergent situations, this is not what they learn in medical schools. The science is coming out and some are open to it and some want to hold on to an outdated model.

You can stent the artery. You can drop the cholesterol. But unless you fix the wall, you haven't fixed the disease.

In the next chapter, we'll dive into what it means to test the artery wall, how to move beyond anatomy and finally start looking at the real cause of heart attacks: inflammation, dysfunction, and vulnerability that most tests still miss.

Because the future of prevention isn't about finding blockages per se. It's about understanding artery biology, before it's too late. It is about stopping the acute event or heart attack.

CHAPTER 6 – What We Should Be Testing (But Usually Don't)

Most of the heart tests we rely on stress tests, calcium scores, angiograms, are designed to find blockages, not biology.

They're built on a plumbing model. And as we've already explored, that model is outdated. It explains some emergencies. But it misses the most important question in prevention, whether you are trying to prevent your first heart attack or next one.

Is this artery vulnerable to rupture, or is it stable and healing?

That's not something you see on a scan. That's something you understand by studying the artery wall itself.

What We've Been Missing

Most fatal heart attacks don't happen to people with obvious warning signs. They don't always have significant blockages. They often don't have sky-high cholesterol. Many don't even have symptoms, until it's too late.

So, what's going wrong?

It turns out, the real danger isn't the size of the blockage or the percentage of narrowing inside an artery. It's what's happening beneath the surface, the underlying biology of the artery wall.

Heart disease doesn't begin with obstruction. It begins with inflammation. It begins when the endothelium, that delicate inner lining of your arteries, becomes dysfunctional. It begins when oxidized lipoproteins irritate the vessel wall, when immune cells are activated inappropriately, when nitric oxide production drops off, and when mechanical stress builds around a vulnerable area of plaque.

These are the real drivers of risk.

They're not always visible on an angiogram. They're not caught by an exercise stresstest. And they don't show up on a basic cholesterol panel. But they're active, dangerous, and often completely silent.

This is what we should be testing. Not just how open your arteries are, but how healthy, how stable, and how biologically protected they really are.

What It Really Means to Test the Artery Wall

When I talk about testing the artery wall, I'm not talking about surgery. No one's opening your chest. This is about something far more meaningful, and far more modern. Remember these arteries are a muscle, not a pipe.

It's about understanding what your arteries are doing, not just what they look like.

Are they flexible or stiff?

Are they inflamed or calm?

Are they silently vulnerable, or actively healing?

We've spent decades asking the wrong question:

"Is there a blockage?" When what we should be asking is: "Is this artery at risk of rupturing?"

Because risk doesn't begin with a blockage. It begins with dysfunction, at the cellular, biological and molecular level.

So, when we talk about "artery wall testing," we're talking about understanding the behavior of your arteries, their biology, their resilience, their early warning signals, well before symptoms or scans can show anything at all.

Let's break down what that looks like.

Endothelial Function — The Early Signal

It all starts with the endothelium, that one-cell-thick lining inside every artery. When it's healthy, the endothelium acts like a smart, responsive barrier. When it's not, it's ground zero for heart disease.

The endothelium is plaque begins to form. It's where inflammation begins. It's where the body decides whether to repair… or to rupture.

Endothelial function testing shows us how

your arteries respond to demand. Are they relaxing and dilating when they should? Or are they stiff, reactive, and slow?

If your endothelium doesn't respond well, that's an early red flag. Even if your cholesterol is fine. Even if your calcium score is zero. Even if your stress test is "normal."

You can't see that dysfunction on an image. But you can measure it, if you know where to look.

Nitric Oxide — The Molecule of Vascular Health

If the endothelium is the command center of your arteries, then nitric oxide is its primary language, and arguably its most powerful tool.

This small gas molecule plays an outsized role in vascular health. When everything is working properly, nitric oxide keeps your arteries smooth, relaxed, and responsive. It dilates your vessels when you need more oxygen. It prevents immune cells and platelets from sticking to the artery wall. It calms inflammation, reduces clot risk, and promotes regeneration of the endothelium itself. In other words, it's central to every function you want a healthy artery to perform.

And yet, most people, and most patients, have never heard of it.

Nitric oxide isn't something that gets mentioned on your stress test report or discussed during a standard cardiology checkup. But the research on it is enormous. In fact, the discovery of nitric oxide's role in the cardiovascular system won the Nobel Prize in 1998. Since then, it has become clear: if nitric oxide is robust, your arteries are protected. If nitric oxide is failing, your arteries are vulnerable, even if your scans and labs look fine.

Where does it come from?

There are two primary ways your body makes nitric oxide. The first is through what you eat, the nitrate–nitrite–nitric oxide (NO) pathway. This is where your diet plays a direct biochemical role. When you consume nitrate-rich vegetables like beets, spinach, arugula, or dark leafy greens, those nitrates get absorbed into your bloodstream, circulate to your salivary glands, and are then secreted into your saliva.

Here's where it gets interesting. Certain bacteria in your mouth, part of your oral microbiome, convert those nitrates into nitrites. When you swallow them, the acidic environment in your stomach, as well as your blood and tissues, convert those nitrites into nitric oxide. It's a naturally elegant system, but it only works if that chain is intact. If you're eating processed foods, using mouthwash, on acid-suppressing medications, or if your oral and gut microbiome is out of balance, you can break that chain. That's how you can eat the right foods and still not make the nitric oxide you need. This is why I often tell patients: your mouth is part of your heart health, and not just metaphorically.

The second pathway is enzymatic. Inside

your blood vessels, the cells that line the arteries, the same endothelial cells that regulate your vascular tone, use an enzyme called eNOS (endothelial nitric oxide synthase) to convert the amino acid L-arginine into nitric oxide. This is the pathway most people associate with supplements. But this system is far more sensitive than most realize. It starts to decline with age and is easily disrupted by oxidative stress, insulin resistance, sedentary behavior, and chronic inflammation. When this pathway is impaired, your arteries lose their ability to respond quickly, and that makes you more susceptible to poor blood flow, high blood pressure, and ultimately, plaque formation.

Now, let's clear up a major misconception.

Many people assume nitric oxide can be "boosted" with a simple supplement. And yes, there are plenty of powders, pills, and pre-workout formulas that make this claim. But nitric oxide isn't a switch you flip, it's a system you support.

I've interviewed some of the top physicians and researchers in the nitric oxide space, and the consensus is clear. Nitric oxide production depends on the health of the entire pathway. If your enzyme system is broken, megadose of arginine won't help. If your oral microbiome is suppressed, drinking beet juice might not move the needle. If your arteries are inflamed, your nitric oxide won't last long even if you produce it.

That's why I often say: nitric oxide is not a quick fix, it's a threshold.

You want to keep your nitric oxide above a

protective threshold, day in and day out. It might mean repairing microbiome function. It might mean cleaning up diet, improving sleep, reducing stress, and using exercise in the right dose and rhythm. Yes, this can absolutely be hacked. But only if you understand how the system works.

Too often, I see patients chasing "Nitric Oxide boosters" that promise performance, when what they really need is balance. When nitric oxide is steady and functional, your arteries are quiet. They're calm. They're responsive. They're not vulnerable to rupture, even if there's some plaque. This is where you can test these levels in your blood with advanced testing.

When nitric oxide is depleted, whether due to aging, stress, inflammation, poor diet, or high blood sugar, everything changes. The arteries get stiff. The lining gets sticky. The immune system gets jumpy. And the foundation is set for vulnerable plaque to build, rupture, and trigger a heart attack.

And here's the thing: you won't know nitric oxide is failing from a stress test. You won't see it on an angiogram. It's invisible to conventional cardiology. But it's central to cardiovascular health.

Thankfully, we can test for it, and we can rebuild it.

If you want to go deeper, I've gathered a number of these expert interviews and resources at heartfit.ca, including insights on testing, interpretation, and what nitric oxide strategies actually work. Because this isn't something you can guess at. It's something you build. And it might be the most powerful cardiovascular tool you've never been told about.

Inflammatory Markers — Listening to the Fire Inside

Most heart attacks are driven by inflammation. It's not the size of the plaque. It's the activity of the immune system in the artery wall that makes it dangerous.

We now have the ability to measure that inflammation, long before a problem shows up on imaging.

Markers like hsCRP (high sensitivity C-Reactive Protein), Lp-PLA2 (lipoprotein-associated phospholipase A2), MPO (Myeloperoxidase), Nitric Oxide at cellular levels and metabolic metabolism such as TMAO (Trimethylamine N -oxide) can tell us if your arteries are getting injured. Is that endothelial lining getting hurt. These aren't fringe metrics. They're used in the research. They just haven't made their way into standard care.

But they should. Because they show us what a stress test is not able to: whether your body is silently building toward a crisis.

Particle Sizes — Getting Smarter About Cholesterol

Cholesterol is still part of the picture, but the type matters far more than the total. The majority of heart attacks occur with people with normal cholesterol profiles. Remember it is not cholesterol that accumulates to a pipe, and you have a last piece of pizza and end up with a heart attack.

Small, dense LDL is more dangerous than large, fluffy LDL. LDL Particle numbers along with apo Lipoprotein B tells us how many particles are floating around; not just how much cholesterol is inside them. Lipoprotein(a) is a genetic variant that increases risk and almost never gets tested. High-Density Lipoprotein (HDL) can also become plaque causing along with Very Low-Density Lipoproteins.

These are the kinds of details that determine whether cholesterol is harmless or harmful. But again, most patients never hear about them.

And if we're serious about prevention, we need to change that. The cure every cardiologist is trained to do is make sure you take your statin, take your drugs to lower cholesterol. It goes beyond cholesterol. As a cholesterol lowering drug or statin only focuses on LDL total. You end up missing everything else that could be vulnerable for getting into the lining of the artery wall.

Plaque Activity — Not All Plaque Is Equal

Plaque is only dangerous when it's unstable. And now we can measure signals that show whether your plaque is leaking, inflamed, or active, especially with newer protein assays that detect vulnerable lesions, looking for that risk of a vulnerable plaque rupture. How active is your immune response to the artery wall? This is vital to understand your cardiovascular disease risk.

These tests don't just say, "you have plaque." They tell us: "this plaque is dangerous and here's how likely it is to rupture."

That's what people want to know. Not just what's there, but what's likely to happen.

Functional vs. Structural Testing

A treadmill stress test tells you what your ECG (Electrocardiogram) looks like when you're walking uphill. An angiogram shows you where the pipe is narrowed.

But none of that tells you:

Whether the artery is actively diseased

Whether plaque is stable or about to rupture. Unless there are more invasive procedures with the angiogram like Intravascular Ultrasound or Optimal Coherence Tomography. But this is damaging the endothelium. Again, risk versus benefit question to ask.

Whether inflammation is driving progression beneath the surface

It's like evaluating a building based on its windows, and ignoring the cracks in the foundation.

That's why we need functional and biochemical testing, not just imaging.

The Power of Early Detection

The biggest breakthroughs in modern medicine didn't come from new treatments. They came from catching things earlier:

Colonoscopy for polyps

Pap smears for cervical changes

Hemoglobin A1C for blood sugar trends

Bone scans for fracture risk

Why not the same for heart disease? We just have to stop pretending cholesterol and stress tests are enough.

We have the ability to detect vulnerable plaque, inflamed arteries, dysfunctional endothelium, years before an event.

A Note on Non-Invasive Testing

There's a misconception that if something's serious, the test should be invasive.

That's not true.

The most powerful testing we have today is non-invasive, radiation-free, and focused on function, not just structure.

And the best part?

These tests can show improvement over time. They help track healing, not just damage.

You don't just want to know what's wrong. You want to know if it's getting better. This is the power of using Artificial Intelligence (AI), scanning the heart with frequency versus duration of the heart. The AI Heart scan is a powerful tool to understand cardiovascular disease risk.

The New Standard in Heart Risk

This is where the conversation needs to go:

Away from "do you have a blockage?"

And toward "how healthy is your vascular biology?"

It's not about running more tests.

It's about running better ones, the kind that show you the full picture, not just a snapshot of a pipe.

Because a clean angiogram doesn't mean you're safe.

And a zero-calcium score doesn't mean you're low risk.

And a negative stress test doesn't mean you're in the clear.

Now that we know what we should be testing, and why, the next chapter will explore what to actually do about it.

Because it's not enough to know you're at risk. You need a path forward, one that's evidence-based, biology-driven, and built for prevention, not procedure.

CHAPTER 7 – What Your Doctor Might Miss

By this point in the book, you've likely begun to see a pattern.

The traditional cardiology model is highly effective in emergencies. If you're having a heart attack, if a vessel is fully blocked, if you're unstable, there is no better place to be than a cath lab with a skilled interventional cardiologist or cardiovascular surgeon. I've seen it save lives. I've been the beneficiary of that system myself.

But what happens when you're not in crisis?

What if your cholesterol is "normal," your stress test came back "clear," your doctor says everything looks "fine" but something still doesn't feel right? That's where the model breaks down.

What if your cholesterol is "high", or your stress test came back "positive", and your doctor says we have to investigate this further. This is where we are following an out-dated model.

Because most physicians, even well-meaning ones, aren't trained to test for what actually matters in prevention. Not because they don't care, but because the system doesn't incentivize it, and the tools they have access to weren't designed for it.

In this chapter, I want to show you what your doctor might miss, and how to think differently when it comes to your own heart. I'll walk you through some common blind spots, and share a few patient stories that illustrate just how easy it is to fall through the cracks.

The Limitations of Standard Care

The average appointment with a general practitioner lasts around 10 to 15 minutes. In that time, they have to review your chart, listen to your symptoms, interpret your labs, renew your medications, and try to address your concerns. That's not enough time to ask deeper questions, especially when the tests they're relying on (cholesterol, ECG, basic blood pressure) all come back "normal."

Cardiologists, for their part, are often trained around crisis management. Their tools, angiograms, stress tests, stents, bypass, are designed to detect or fix obstructive, late-stage disease. They're not designed to catch the biology of early plaque formation, endothelial dysfunction, or immune dysregulation. They're trained to identify and treat plumbing issues, not subtle instability inside the artery wall.

That's not a knock. It's just how the system works.

And this is where smart, proactive patients, people like you, can get lost. Because if the test says "you're fine," and the symptoms aren't classic, you're often reassured and sent home.

Mrs. Evelyn — "You're Fine... Until You're Not"

Mrs. Evelyn was 59. Fit, energetic, recently retired. She walked her dog twice a day, cooked most of her meals, didn't smoke, and had no family history of heart disease. When she started to feel occasional tightness in her chest on cold mornings, she did the right thing: she went to her doctor.

Her cholesterol was well within normal limits. Blood pressure: excellent. ECG: normal. The doctor smiled and said what we've all heard too many times:

"Everything looks good. It's probably stress (anxiety)."

Still, Evelyn pushed. She asked for a stress test. They gave her a treadmill ECG, which she passed. No symptoms. No changes.

She went home relieved.

Three months later, Evelyn had a heart attack while shoveling snow. It wasn't the "big one," but it was enough to scare her, and it was enough to damage her heart. When the angiogram was done post-event, it showed moderate disease with vulnerable plaque rupture in an artery that hadn't looked obstructive on any prior testing.

Her risk wasn't from a tight blockage. It was from unstable biology inside the artery wall, the kind of thing no traditional test picked up.

Evelyn didn't fail the system. The system

failed her.

Mr. Michael — "What If We Hadn't Looked?"

Mr. Michael was 47. He came to our clinic not because he had symptoms, but because a friend of his had dropped dead of a heart attack at 51. No warning. No signs. It shook him.

His doctor told him not to worry. Michael was a runner. His LDL was 2.5 mmol/L (around 100 mg/dL). His blood pressure was great. No family history.

Still, he had that gut feeling. So, we ran a full assessment, not a stress test, not a cholesterol panel, but a biological scan of his artery function.

We looked at his artery health like it should be done in prevention. We looked at the artery function and the biology of the artery wall, because it is a muscle not a pipe.

What we found shocked him. He had significant endothelial dysfunction, high Lp(a), and an elevated plaque rupture test, indicating his artery wall was leaking inflammatory proteins, a sign of vulnerable plaque ready to pop.

Had he waited for symptoms, or relied on a traditional stress test, that risk would've been invisible.

Instead, we started him on a personalized program: targeted lifestyle changes, precision medical therapy, and non-invasive treatment to improve his vascular function. Today, he's still running, and he has peace of mind not because he "passed a test," but because we actually addressed the root cause.

Mr. Ravi — When "Positive" Still Doesn't Mean Emergency

Mr. Ravi was a 61-year-old man with type 2 diabetes, well controlled, active, lean, and on top of his health. He didn't smoke, watched his diet, and came in to see us because of mild chest discomfort on exertion. He wanted to be proactive, not reactive.

His doctor sent him for a stress test. It came back positive, ECG changes consistent with ischemia. That triggered the usual next step: a referral for invasive coronary angiography.

This was exactly where patients get funneled down a one-way street, especially if no one steps back to ask: What does this test really mean?

This was the kind of case that the ISCHEMIA trial was built around. A patient with symptoms. A positive stress test. But no unstable disease. The trial taught us that jumping to angiography and stenting in these patients doesn't improve outcomes. Optimal medical therapy and lifestyle intervention are not just sufficient, they are, in many cases, superior.

But as I've said earlier in this book, cardiologists are trained not to tolerate ischemia. So, Ravi's positive test led him to the cath lab.

Now, I have had many patients stop at a failed

stress test. There is no need for further radiation, dyes, and angiograms, as we already know. It is time to follow the trials and start with optimal medical therapy along referring to cardiac rehabilitation, External Counterpulsation, Hydrogen therapy along with understanding their personalized biology of the artery wall.

Mr. Ravi s angiogram showed moderate disease, not tight enough to stent, but not squeaky clean either. But he still had symptoms.

This is a classic and often overlooked diagnosis: microvascular angina. It doesn't show up on a standard angiogram because it doesn't involve large vessel blockages. It's a problem of small arteries, the microvasculature, where endothelial dysfunction and poor nitric oxide signaling prevent proper dilation during stress.

The only way to truly see it is with a functional angiogram, sometimes involving injection of acetylcholine to assess how the arteries respond under provocation. But that's rarely done. Instead, these patients are often told "there's nothing wrong", even though they still don't feel right.

That's when Ravi came back to us.

We didn't stop at anatomy. We tested his artery wall biology, his endothelial function, inflammatory markers, and oxidative stress load. We confirmed what his angiogram couldn't show: he had vascular dysfunction.

Therefore, we treated the real problem.

We started him on a targeted, biology-based plan: improving his nitric oxide pathways, reducing arterial inflammation, and beginning a course of External Counterpulsation (ECP) therapy, a non-invasive treatment shown to improve microvascular flow and artery function.

Weeks later, his symptoms had diminished. His function improved. And most importantly, he understood what was happening in his body, and how to stay ahead of it.

The Patient Who "Passed" — and Almost Didn't Survive

There's another story I should to share, one I've told before in clinical settings, and one that never leaves me.

It was a patient we followed closely. He'd gone for a routine treadmill stress test because of some mild shortness of breath while hiking. The test was negative. In fact, the cardiologist's report described it as an "excellent result", reassuring heart rate response, no ECG changes, no concerning symptoms.

He was told what so many people are told:

"Your test is normal. You're fine. Keep up the good work."

But weeks later, he collapsed at home. Emergency services rushed him to the hospital. He'd had a heart attack, one caused by a ruptured plaque in an artery that had shown no significant narrowing on the stress test.

When we reviewed his case, it was clear what had happened. The plaque that triggered his heart attack wasn't obstructive, it didn't limit flow during exercise. But it was unstable, inflamed, and vulnerable. And the test he was given wasn't designed to detect that.

That patient survived. Barely. And only because everything aligned in the emergency response, rapid ambulance arrival, fast thrombolytics, and a skilled team.

But what struck me most was how close he came to being another "normal test, sudden death" statistic. The system did what it was trained to do. It followed protocol. But protocol didn't look deep enough.

The New Path Forward

These aren't rare stories. They're everywhere. And they make one thing clear: if we want to reduce heart attacks, we need to move beyond comfort phrases like "everything looks fine." We need to look deeper, at the biology, not just the plumbing.

Because you don't prevent a fire by checking if the house is currently burning. You prevent it by inspecting the wiring, understanding the risk, and fixing what can't be seen with the naked eye.

This isn't about doing nothing. It's about doing the right thing, with better tools, better strategy, and better understanding.

In the next chapter, I'll show you what that testing looks like, and how we can catch the cracks in the system before they become catastrophe.

CHAPTER 8 – Better Testing, Better Prevention

For decades, we've asked the wrong question:

"Is there a blockage?"

But heart attacks don't start with a 90% to 95% blockage. They start with inflammation, dysfunction, and instability in the artery wall, long before the artery narrows. So, if we want to prevent heart attacks, we need to stop focusing on obstruction and start asking a better question:

How healthy is your artery wall?

Because the truth is, most heart attacks happen in people who would have "passed" the conventional tests. Normal cholesterol. Normal stress test. Clean CT scan. And yet... they collapse on a jog, or don't wake up from sleep, or clutch their chest in the middle of an ordinary day.

It's not the blockage. It's the biology.

And if we're going to change outcomes, we need to test what actually matters.

What Should We Be Testing Instead?

We need to shift from testing the "plumbing" to understanding the vascular biology, the forces and factors that make arteries resilient or rupture-prone.

This includes:

1. Endothelial Function

This is ground zero for cardiovascular health. The endothelium is the inner lining of your blood vessels, only one cell thick, and it controls everything from dilation and contraction to inflammation and immune signaling.

A healthy endothelium produces nitric oxide, maintains smooth blood flow, and resists plaque formation. A dysfunctional endothelium becomes sticky, inflamed, and prone to clot-triggering events.

Tests that assess flow-mediated dilation, pulse wave velocity, or reactive hyperemia can give early, non-invasive insights into this function, long before symptoms appear.

2. Inflammatory Markers and Immune Activation

Heart disease is an inflammatory condition. And yet, the standard lipid panel tells us nothing about inflammation. We should be measuring high-sensitivity CRP, MPO, Lp-PLA2, and even interleukins when appropriate.

Some newer tools like the plaque rupture testing, measure the actual proteins released when plaque becomes vulnerable. That's not a guess. That's biology in action.

3. Lipoprotein Particle Profiles

I remember a patient, mid-50s, clean lifestyle, no symptoms, and proud of his "perfect cholesterol numbers." His total LDL was 2.3 mmol/L. He figured he was in the clear. But when we dug deeper, what we found told a different story.

I explained it like this: total cholesterol is like measuring the volume of traffic on a freeway. It gives you a number, how many lipoprotein particles are circulating. But it tells you nothing about what kind of traffic you're dealing with. That's where particle size comes in.

Imagine two people with the same total LDL level. One has mostly large, fluffy particles, think tennis balls. The other has small, dense ones, think golf balls. The golf balls can slip through the cracks, penetrate the endothelium, oxidize, and trigger an immune response. That's where the damage begins. That's what sets the stage for plaque rupture and heart attack.

This patient, despite a "normal" LDL, had an overwhelming number of small, dense LDL particles. He was a walking example of why standard cholesterol tests miss the mark, and why understanding lipoprotein profiles matters so much more than a single number.

What matters is the size and density of the particles — small, dense LDL is far more dangerous than large, fluffy LDL. Apolipoprotein B can tell us how many atherogenic particles are circulating. What is more important is to understand how many small LDL particles you have. Lp(a) — lipoprotein(a) is one of the most underrecognized, genetically driven risk factors.

It is also important to understand VLDL (Very Low-Density Lipoprotein) and High Density Lipoprotein (HDL) sizing along. Yes, even good cholesterol can be deceptive, It has to function well as good cholesterol. Again, it is about having large fluffy functional HDL cholesterol.

If you're not looking at these, you're not seeing the full picture. What becomes more important is to make sure we minimize the plaque building process with these plaque building particles.

4. Arterial Wall Imaging

Tools like Carotid Intima-Media Thickness (CIMT) give us a look at the thickness and stability of the artery wall, not just the lumen. It's like inspecting the wall of a tire, not just checking the air pressure.

Unlike calcium scores, CIMT can show you the early changes: soft plaque, wall thickening, endothelial swelling. These are the earliest signs of risk. And they're modifiable.

5. Electrical and Recovery-Based Markers

Even heart rate variability (HRV) and autonomic testing can give us insight into the stress and resilience of the cardiovascular system. Your nervous system plays a role in arterial health too, especially in high-stress, high-cortisol states.

Real Patients, Real Clarity

Let me tell you about Susan.

She was 52, fit, and had just "passed" her annual medical. Normal cholesterol. Normal ECG. She even did a treadmill stress test, and her doctor said, "You're great. Keep doing what you're doing."

Two months later, she felt a wave of fatigue during a hike. No chest pain. No crushing symptoms. Just off. She listened to her body and came to us. Her CIMT showed thickening and early plaque. Her endothelial function was impaired. Her inflammation markers were high. She wasn't "fine." She was on the edge.

We treated her biology, not her cholesterol, and six months later, her arterial health had transformed.

Then there's Malik.

A 61-year-old with diabetes, referred to us after a positive stress test. The cardiologist recommended a coronary angiogram. He wasn't thrilled about going down that road. We looked deeper.

His biology was inflamed. His arterial elasticity was poor. His plaque was active but not obstructive. He had microvascular angina, the kind that doesn't show up on an angiogram. We started him on optimal therapy, dialed in his lifestyle, and used ECP to improve perfusion. His symptoms resolved, no stent required.

Even if there was a significant blockage doing ECP, hydrogen therapy and attending to the biology of the artery wall will reverse heart disease way better than putting in a heart stent or bypass surgery. This is only for that person who has stable advanced heart disease. If it is an emergency, and it is a heart attack best to be there as soon as you can as seeing a cardiologist is life saving.

A Shift in Standards

This kind of testing isn't futuristic. It's here. It's validated. And it's what should be standard, if our goal is prevention.

Unfortunately, insurance rarely pays for it. Institutions don't teach it. And most physicians don't have time to learn it. So instead, we use what's reimbursed. What's fast. What's familiar.

That's the gap. Not a knowledge gap, a systems gap. But that gap is where most heart attacks happen.

From Outdated to Proactive

We can keep waiting for the stress test to change, or we can change how we test.

The future of heart health is already here. We just need to look beyond the blockage and start asking what the artery is telling us. Not just how open it is, but how stable, how functional, how alive it is.

Because arteries aren't pipes. And we can't fix what we don't test for.

CHAPTER 9 – Beyond Statins and Surgery

For too long, the dominant approach to heart disease has been this: lower cholesterol, stent blockages, repeat.

It's a model built on numbers, not nuance. On plumbing, not biology. On reacting to visible damage, instead of understanding why the damage happened in the first place.

And yet, despite all of our drugs, procedures, and technology, heart disease remains the number one killer worldwide.

So maybe it's time we ask the question: What if we've been managing the wrong thing all along?

A Reflex, Not a Reason

It's nearly automatic. You walk into a clinic with slightly elevated LDL, or a family history, or you're a man or women over 50. Out comes the prescription pad: statin.

No conversation about diet. No exploration of lifestyle. No assessment of inflammation, insulin resistance, nitric oxide function, or nutrient status. Just a reflex. A statin.

This isn't a conspiracy, it's training. Medical school, guidelines, CM (Continuing Medical Education) modules, all have drilled in the idea that cholesterol is the villain and statins are the savior.

The lower the LDL, the better. End of story.

But that story is incomplete. And in many cases, it's wrong.

The History of a Myth

The war on cholesterol began in the 1970s, when pathologists dissected arteries and found cholesterol in the plaque. The logic seemed straightforward: cholesterols in the plaque, so let's get rid of cholesterol.

By the time pharmaceutical companies had developed statins to block the body's cholesterol production, public messaging had already taken hold. TIME Magazine covers, Maclean's articles, government guidelines, all declared war on fat and cholesterol. And thus, the low-fat, low-cholesterol, high-carb era was born.

Butter became dangerous. Eggs became a warning sign. Bagels and "heart healthy" cereal? Green-lighted.

The food industry pivoted hard to "low-fat," the pharmaceutical industry doubled down on statins, and we entered a generation of metabolic dysfunction.

We're now seeing the cost: more diabetes, more obesity, and more heart disease than ever.

Statins: What the Data Really Says

To be clear, statins have a role, especially in secondary prevention. If you've had a heart attack or stroke, they can help reduce the chance of another one. But the degree of benefit depends entirely on your risk.

Let's talk about NNT — Number Needed to Treat.

In high-risk populations, statins prevent a heart attack or death in about 1 out of every 30–40 people over five years. That's significant. But that is also hoping to hit a number on the roulette table. It is a gamble.

But in primary prevention, meaning patients with no history of cardiovascular events, the NNT climbs to 100–150 or more. That means for every 100 people who take a statin for five years, one person avoids a heart attack. The other 99 take on the cost, inconvenience, and potential side effects... for nothing. We are now hoping for a lottery.

Then came the FOURIER trial, which dropped LDL by 74% using a PCSK9 inhibitor, a more powerful cousin to statins. Sounds amazing, right? But the actual absolute risk reduction was 1.5%. A multi-billion-dollar therapy, and 98.5% of people saw no clinical benefit.

This is the difference between relative risk reduction (which sounds impressive) and absolute risk reduction (which is what actually matters to you as a person).

And yet, statins remain the first-line treatment, not because the outcomes are spectacular, but because they move the needle on a lab value.

The Cost of Chasing Numbers

Cholesterol is not the enemy. It's a vital molecule, essential for hormone production, cell membrane integrity, neurological health, immune regulation, and tissue repair. Lowering it indiscriminately has consequences.

Statins inhibit the production of Coenzyme Q10, which powers mitochondria, the energy centers of your cells. Many patients experience fatigue, muscle pain, or cognitive decline. Some notice sleep disturbances, mood changes, or insulin resistance.

They also impair vitamin K2 metabolism, a nutrient critical for keeping calcium in your bones and out of your arteries.

When we treat cholesterol in isolation, without considering why it's elevated, or how it's behaving, we risk doing harm in the name of prevention.

The Case for Smarter Medicine

Not all LDL is created equal. The large, buoyant particles? Less dangerous. The small, dense ones? Highly inflammatory. But standard lipid panels don't show that.

More meaningful tests, like ApoB, Lp(a), oxidized LDL, and advanced lipoprotein profiles, give a better picture of risk. But most patients never get them. Because they're not standard. Because they're not covered. Because we've prioritized simplicity over specificity.

And when that patient returns with a "normal" LDL but is still at risk, the system has no answer. Because the real danger isn't the cholesterol. It's the inflammation, endothelial dysfunction, immune activation, oxidative stress, and arterial vulnerability.

That's where the focus should be.

A Better Path for Stable Patients

If you've already had a heart attack, yes, consider statins. But don't stop there.

If you haven't had a cardiac event but have risk factors, the solution isn't to medicate blindly. It's to investigate thoroughly.

That means:

Addressing inflammation

Testing artery function and biology

Measuring endothelial health

Correcting micronutrient deficiencies

Improving nitric oxide production

Supporting the gut and metabolic system

Because heart disease is systemic, not just local to a blockage.

What About Procedures?

It's tempting to believe that a stent "fixes" heart disease. But for stable coronary artery disease, the evidence is clear:

The COURAGE Trial showed no reduction in heart attacks or death with stenting versus optimal medical therapy.

The ORBITA Trial, a sham-controlled study, showed no difference in symptoms between patients who received a stent and those who didn't, therefore highlighting the placebo effect of procedures.

The ISCHEMIA Trial, one of the most important in recent years, confirmed that in moderate-to-severe ischemia, there was no benefit from early intervention over medical therapy, except for symptom relief in certain patients.

Procedures can be powerful. But they're not prevention.

They don't stabilize plaque. They don't improve arterial biology. They don't treat the cause. They treat the result.

The Role of Cardiac Rehab and ECP Therapy

If you truly want to reverse heart disease, not just delay its consequences, you need a foundation rooted in lifestyle and biology-based care.

Cardiac rehabilitation is one of the most clinically validated, yet underutilized, treatments in cardiology. Despite decades of evidence showing, it reduces death, hospital readmission, and improves quality of life, referral rates remain shockingly low. Many patients are discharged after a cardiac event with a prescription for medication, but no structured support for behavior change, physical activity, or recovery.

When done properly, cardiac rehab is not just exercise. It's a guided reset: education, nutrition, stress management, emotional support, risk factor modification, the very tools that treat the root causes of coronary artery disease, not just its symptoms.

And yet, even cardiac rehab isn't the full picture.

Enter ECP therapy, External Counterpulsation. A non-invasive, rhythm-synchronized treatment that uses pneumatic cuffs on the legs to increase coronary perfusion during diastole. Think of it as a way to supercharge blood flow to the heart — while the heart is resting.

Over time, this increased flow stimulates collateral vessel formation (the heart's natural bypass system), improves endothelial function, reduces anginal symptoms, enhances VO_2 max, and supports microvascular circulation, especially in patients where blockages aren't visible, but dysfunction is real.

ECP is FDA-approved. Supported by numerous clinical trials. Safe. Painless. Often life-changing.

Yet many cardiologists either don't offer it, don't understand it, or still consider it a "last resort."

Why?

Because it doesn't fit the old model. It doesn't

involve stents. It doesn't require an OR. It doesn't generate the same revenue in a fee-for-service system. And it challenges the conventional belief that coronary artery disease can only be managed by fixing blockages.

But CAD isn't just about blockages. It's about biology, inflammation, endothelial dysfunction, microvascular impairment, and this is exactly where ECP excels, along with hydrogen therapy.

ECP should not be a backup plan. It should be a first-line option for patients with stable CAD, especially those with microvascular angina, diffuse disease, or those who've already had procedures and are still symptomatic.

It's time we stop treating this therapy as a niche intervention and start recognizing it as one of the most powerful, underused tools in cardiovascular medicine. When combined with cardiac rehab and optimal medical therapy, ECP represents a modern, patient-centered approach to treating heart disease, one that heals from the inside out.

Not because we "couldn't do a stent."

But because we never needed one in the first place.

What Patients Deserve

You deserve more than a prescription.

You deserve a conversation about your goals, your biology, your lifestyle.

You deserve testing that looks at how your arteries function, not just how narrow they are.

You deserve prevention that works.

Statins might be part of that equation. But they should never be the default. Not without a full picture of your vascular health. Not without understanding the trade-offs. And certainly not without trying everything else first.

Because the truth is: lowering cholesterol is easy. Changing outcomes is harder.

But it's possible, and it starts by shifting the question from "How low can we get the LDL?" to "How healthy can we get the artery?"

CHAPTER 10 – The Emergency Department Trap

The most common reason people visit an emergency department is chest pain.

The most common fear? A heart attack.

It makes sense, chest discomfort is frightening. For the patient, it feels urgent. For the physician, it feels risky. The fear of missing something is enormous. So, what do we do? We rule out the worst-case scenario: a heart attack. And most of the time, that's where the real work should end.

But it doesn't.

Instead, we fall into a familiar trap: the treadmill stress test.

The Patient Pathway That Almost Everyone Follows

It goes like this: a patient walks into the emergency department with chest pain. They're hooked up to a monitor, have blood drawn, and get an ECG. If they're not actively having a heart attack, meaning their ECG is normal and their troponin levels are stable, they're ruled out for an acute event.

They're relieved. But they're not done.

They're discharged with a referral to a

cardiologist, or worse, a request for a "non-urgent stress test."

And that's where the detour begins.

Instead of focusing on long-term risk, underlying biology, or meaningful lifestyle changes, we reroute them toward imaging. Toward procedures. Toward radiation. We prioritize seeing the plumbing, even when the pipes look fine.

A Case That Tells the Whole Story

Let me tell you about one of our patients, a diabetic, relatively well-controlled, with no previous heart disease but some vague chest symptoms that started under stress.

His emergency department workup was negative. ECG normal. Troponins normal. He was referred for a treadmill stress test, which came back "positive." That led to a nuclear stress test, also positive. He was now scared and scheduled for an angiogram.

And here's what they found: moderate disease. No culprit lesion. No blockage requiring a stent. He was told it wasn't bad enough to intervene... and sent home.

No real treatment plan. No understanding of why he was experiencing symptoms. No conversation about microvascular disease, despite being diabetic, which puts him at higher risk for small vessel dysfunction.

This was a textbook example of the

ISCHEMIA trial in action, and in defiance. That trial, which randomized over 5,000 patients with abnormal stress tests, found that in stable cases like this one, invasive testing and procedures offered no benefit over optimal medical therapy.

Still, the system ignored it.

We brought him into the clinic, assessed his artery biology, and confirmed that his symptoms likely stemmed from endothelial dysfunction and microvascular angina. We started him on a personalized treatment plan, including ECP therapy, a proven approach to improve small vessel function, increase perfusion, and reduce symptoms. We tracked his biology. His symptoms resolved.

But none of that would have happened if he had just followed the system's usual path, which stops at anatomy and never gets to function.

Why Are We Still Stress Testing in the Emergency Department?

The truth is, emergency departments are overwhelmed and oversensitive to risk. No one wants to miss a heart attack. But once that heart attack is ruled out, the risk of a subsequent event, in a patient with normal ECG and normal troponins, is incredibly low.

Study after study has confirmed this. After a negative Emergency Department workup, the risk of having a heart attack in the next 30 days is less than 1 in 1,000. Some studies peg it even lower.

So, what's the harm in a follow-up stress test?

Well, here's what happens when we order one:

Most come back "normal" but offer false reassurance for those with early disease.

Many come back "abnormal" but trigger a cascade of radiation-heavy imaging, invasive procedures, and unnecessary worry.

Very few change outcomes. Almost none identify patients who actually need stents or surgery.

The POPE trial, FOY 2015, Sandhu 2017, and dozens of others all point to the same conclusion: stress testing low-risk Emergency Department patients doesn't reduce heart attacks. It doesn't reduce deaths. But it increases costs, hospital stays, anxiety, radiation exposure, and iatrogenic harm.

Partial Verification Bias: The Hidden Flaw

Part of the illusion of benefit comes from something called partial verification bias. If you fail a stress test, you're sent for more testing, angiograms, usually. And if the angiogram finds disease, we assume the stress test worked.

But if you pass the test, you go home, and we never confirm whether the test was truly right or wrong. We assume it was. And that's how the stress test gains a reputation it doesn't deserve.

Worse, it leads to what I call procedural inertia, when patients get procedures not because they're necessary, but because each test nudges the next one forward. By the time someone gets a stent, no one remembers that the whole journey started with a test that was never needed in the first place.

The Data Doctors Don't See

Despite years of data, COURAGE, ORBITA, ISCHEMIA, and others, the reflex to treat based on testing, not symptoms or biology, remains. Why?

Because cardiologists are trained to intervene. As I've said before: they're trained to not tolerate ischemia. It makes sense in emergencies. But in stable, low-risk patients? It's misapplied.

Take the Sandhu study - over 900,000 Emergency Department patients analyzed. Those who presented on weekdays were more likely to get stress tests (because the lab was open). They were also more likely to get angiograms. But there was no difference in outcomes. None.

They didn't live longer. They didn't avoid more heart attacks. They just got tested more.

What Should Happen Instead

When someone leaves the Emergency Department after a negative cardiac workup, the next steps shouldn't be imaging, they should be biology.

We need to shift from: "Do you have blockages?" To: "Why did your arteries react this way? What is your actual heart attack or stroke risk? How is your artery function? Is your plaque stable or vulnerable to rupture? "

This means smarter testing: understanding ischemia (lack of blood flow), artery health and function, inflammatory markers, plaque activity, and nitric oxide signaling.

It means smarter treatment: lifestyle intervention, optimal medical therapy, ECP therapy.

And above all, it means smarter systems, where prevention is personalized, not protocolized.

Closing Thought

The emergency department is one of the most important safety nets in medicine. But it was never designed to be your preventive care provider.

It rules out what's dangerous today, not what could hurt you tomorrow.

So, the next time someone tells you to "follow up with a stress test," stop and ask:

What are we really looking for?

What are we really preventing?

And what's the next best step, for you?

EPILOGUE – A New Standard of Care

Yes, you already sense it: something should change.

Not just for patients, but for practitioners, policymakers, insurers, and the entire infrastructure of modern cardiology. We've spent decades chasing risk in all the wrong ways, mistaking cholesterol for the enemy, using stress tests to reassure when they should be warning, and intervening with stents and surgery as if the disease were mechanical, when it's mostly biological.

At the Heart Fit Clinic, we've built a new way forward. And while this book isn't about promoting any one clinic, it's impossible not to share the core philosophy that drives our work.

It begins with understanding that cholesterol, in and of itself, does not cause heart disease. That message alone can be disorienting to some, after all, it's been baked into public health campaigns, guidelines, and dinner table conversations for generations. But the science tells a different story. Most people who suffer a heart attack have cholesterol levels in the "normal" range. The real issue isn't how much cholesterol you have, it's what your body is doing with it. Inflammation, oxidation, infection response, immune dysfunction, these are the true culprits. Cholesterol is just caught in the crossfire.

Second, we've come to accept stress tests as the gatekeepers of heart health. You walk the treadmill, the monitor doesn't blare, and you're told you're fine. But the reality is sobering: the majority of heart attacks happen in arteries that were less than 50% blocked, far below the detection threshold of a stress test. It's not that stress testing has no place; it's that we've misused it. We've relied on it to rule out heart disease, when in fact, it often misses the very kind of plaque that ruptures and causes sudden death.

Finally, we need to confront a hard truth: stents and bypass surgery are not a cure. They are powerful interventions in moments of crisis, but they do not prevent future heart attacks in stable patients. And yet, too often, patients leave the hospital believing the disease has been "fixed." What they haven't been told is that unless the biology of their artery walls changes, unless the inflammation calms, the endothelial function improves, and the vulnerable plaque stabilizes, the risk remains.

These are not fringe ideas. They are supported by decades of research, major clinical trials, and real-world outcomes. But they haven't yet made their way into routine care. Not because the science is lacking, but because systems are slow to evolve. Training lags behind evidence. Incentives don't always align with long-term prevention. And too many people are afraid to ask: is there a better way?

There is.

And it starts with asking better questions,

using smarter testing, and seeing the artery not as a pipe to be patched, but as a living organ to be nourished and protected.

You only get one heart. And a clean test doesn't mean a clean bill of health.

This book was written to help you see the blind spots, challenge assumptions, and take control of your cardiovascular future, not through fear, but through understanding.

The old model is broken.

It's time to build a new one.

The Heart Fit Clinic Approach

If this book left you asking, "So what now?" that's exactly the question the Heart Fit Clinic was built to answer.

We don't exist to replace your cardiologist. We're here to fill the gaps, to go where conventional care often stops. And our approach rests on three foundational truths that, once understood, change everything:

1. Cholesterol does not cause heart disease.

Cholesterol is a passenger, not the driver. The science is clear: people with normal cholesterol levels suffer heart attacks all the time. Why? Because it's not just about how much cholesterol is present, it's about how that cholesterol behaves in the artery wall. Inflammation, oxidation, immune activation, these are the forces we should be testing for, tracking, and treating.

2. Most heart attacks occur with blockages under 50%.

This is the most underappreciated reality in cardiology. Stress tests, the gold standard in most medical offices, only detect large, flow-limiting blockages. They miss the vulnerable plaque, the biological instability, the smoldering inflammation that causes over 80% of fatal heart events. That's why a "normal" test result should never be the end of the story.

3. Stents and surgery are not a cure.

They're powerful tools in an emergency. But they don't fix the root cause. If you've had a stent or bypass, your journey isn't over, it's just begun. And if you haven't had an event yet, those procedures won't prevent one. The only way forward is to change the biology of the artery wall, improve function, and reduce the forces that lead to rupture and clot.

At the Heart Fit Clinic, we take that seriously. Our testing looks deeper. Our treatments go further. And our patients learn to stop fearing their heart, and start understanding it.

Because when you know what actually causes heart disease, you realize: you have far more control than you've been led to believe. Please connect with us to understand your artery health further and understand precision medicine with precision nutrition and supplementation based on ones deficiencies.

I've been given the gift of a second life. It began the moment I realized I only get one. That realization continues to drive me not just to help people live longer, but to help them live healthier.

Every week, I meet people who are scared. They've been told they're fine, or they've been rushed into procedures, or they've lost someone they love without warning. And when they come to me, it's never just about numbers or tests, It is about wanting to be here. Wanting to keep doing the things they love, with the people they love.

That's why I do this work. My mission is to inspire and empower through transformative ideas so that what is possible is realized. Realize your full vision and thank you for sharing this journey with me.

Not near one of our clinics? No problem.

I've built Heart Fit University | Heart Health
Education & Support to give you free access to the
tools, insights, and support you need — from a heart
risk quiz to educational videos, supplement
guidance, and more.

Visit Heart Fit University | Heart Health Education
& Support and start making smarter decisions about
your heart health today

AUTHOR'S BIO

Diamond Fernandes is an internationally recognized leader in cardiovascular prevention and rehabilitation. He is the founder of the Heart Fit Clinic, with locations across Canada, and the author of Beating Heart Disease. Over the past two decades, he has helped thousands of patients avoid unnecessary surgery and take control of their heart health through precision testing, education, and lifestyle medicine.

A passionate advocate for patient empowerment, Diamond blends science, clinical experience, and disruptive thinking to challenge the status quo, and build a new standard of care.

www.ingramcontent.com/pod-product-compliance
Lightning Source LLC
Chambersburg PA
CBHW040756220326
41597CB00029BB/4951